MW00941367

LOVE
SEARCH

By
Polly Sanders-Peterson

Love Search
by Polly Sanders-Peterson

Printed in the United States of America

ISBN 978-1-60477-702-4

Unless otherwise indicated, Bible quotations are taken from The Living Bible. Copyright © 1971 by Tyndale House Publishers.

www.xulonpress.com

Chapter titles...

Foreword

Dear Readers...

Have you ever suffered hidden hurts, physical and sexual abuse, rejection, abandonment, woundedness, and—through it all—your most passionate and constant cry was, "I just want to be loved?" Polly Sanders-Peterson's book, *Love Search,* is a story about one woman's life-long journey for love and the valuable lessons she learned along the way. This book doesn't pull any punches; it's an honest, revealing account of how her search led her directly into the arms of God. Read her story and find God's awesome healing power for your life, too!

—Marilyn Hickey
Marilyn Hickey Ministries

Introduction

*All of my life all I ever wanted was to be loved, feel
loved, experience love and acceptance. My eyes still
hold un-spilled tears as I place these feelings on the
computer page. I started writing about this journey
ten years ago. Today, it is in your hand.*

In these next few paragraphs, I have set out a brief outline
of my life *history* so that you can get a feeling for the
person who is telling you this true story. I hope that you
can see that I'm just like you—with a track record of life's
events that have brought me to where I am today—and like
you, I'm still truckin' along on that journey.

Born in the small town of Newport, Arkansas—90 miles
north of Little Rock—I grew up *feeling* unloved, unwanted,
abandoned, rejected and unworthy, always yearning for
someone or something to come along who would love me
and fill that deep hunger in my heart...quite a contrast to
the postcard-perfect countryside that surrounded me with its
layer-upon-layer of deep green forest beauty.

I was the ninth of twelve children, and the oldest of the
four children left at home. My Father, Kirk, was sixty-five
years old when I was born and my Mother, Demore, was

thirty-one. Our home was very small, built up on wooden stilts, one bedroom with no indoor bathroom or electricity, and located in a farming/ranch/pasture area, where cows grazed all around us. We all had chores and mine was doing the family laundry. One day while I hung the sheets on the outside lines, I realized the house was on fire. My Mother, who was very ill, and my youngest brother were inside. I wrapped a blanket around my head and rushed in, pulling them both to safety. Not long after that my Father died, and my Mother was hospitalized in a mental institution, leaving no adult in our home. That's when the four of us younger children went to live with our older siblings. I was sent to Denver, Colorado, to stay with my sister, Diane.

Once settled in Denver, I briefly attended *Cole Middle School,* then *Baker Junior High School* and *East High School,* where I dreamed of becoming a Flight Attendant. Right after graduation I went to the *Hollywood Beauty College* becoming their first African-American student. Soon I met and married James Sanders, and our son, Bryan came into our lives. What a joy! I continued to work as a hair stylist, and eventually invested in a partnership to open a hair salon in the prestigious Cherry Creek shopping district. The business faltered, and my marriage was increasingly difficult as I dealt with physical and mental abuse. Finally, I divorced Mr. Sanders.

With a tiny morsel of renewed confidence, I opened a hair salon on my own and in 1986 won the Madam C.J. Walker *Salon of the Year* award. Life looked a lot better, and I met and married Ray Peterson…who has completed my life in many ways, but he too, brought me even greater challenges.

WHAT THESE FACTS have not revealed is the wounded and bleeding woman who, through all these events in her life, still kept looking on the *outside* for someone or something to fill that gaping void on her *insides.* No matter how many successes I obtained, they never came close to filling that emptiness. Every time I felt low, lonely, or experienced a lack of affection, I would seek a sexual relationship, or reach for a drink, only to discover it was just a temporary fix. Like putting a bandage over an open sore and discovering the pain is still there...or... filling my car with gas, and watching the fuel gauge move toward empty, whatever I did never filled *me*. I still had a desperate need to be whole on the inside...and I cried out for love and acceptance.

On the following pages I have told my story. There are also *lesson bites* at the end of each chapter, gleanings that I have chewed and spit out and chewed again until I understood them and they became palatable and nurturing to my soul. I hope that you will find them useful in your *life's journey*, too.

All my love,   Polly Ann

Beginnings

My early years filter in and out of my memory like film-clips. One of those most in focus was when I was eight years old. My thin little legs stretched up and held me on tiptoes as I reached to hang sheets on the line. The dusty fields of cotton that surrounded our clapboard home waved in a gentle breeze. The sun was hot on my skin. I noticed the smell of smoke, but it seemed natural, so I hung the next piece of laundry. Then—almost in the same instant—I *knew* that our house was on fire. My Mother was inside…helpless…sick and weak and unable to speak. One of my little brothers was with her.

I can still feel the rough blanket that I wrapped around my upper body and head. It smothered me, but at the same time protected me as I rushed into the house. Then we were outside. I don't remember being inside the house, or how I got both my Mother and brother out, but there we were, sitting on the ground, watching the flames slice through the windows. I have no recollection of other people showing up, but somehow all three of us were safe outside.

AS FAR BACK as I can remember I always had a lot of responsibility. I was born in mid-1944, and grew up as the ninth of twelve children. While people in the United States tried to balance the effects of WWII, and children of London England dodged German bombs, I played in the Arkansas cotton and corn fields with my friends and my three younger brothers. Even though I'm certain that the adults in our family experienced these *war years* in a much different way than I did, I played and went to school, and worked hard— very hard. Before I was 10 years old I *knew* that I had to help hold the family together and *together* I held it! So off I went...not only doing household chores, but also working outside the home in the cotton fields—and boy, I could pick some cotton!

My father, Curtis "Kirk" Rucker, was 65 years old when I was born and my mother, Demore, was 31. I remember my Mom's sister (Aunt Madie) telling me how they met my Dad. One Sunday afternoon, my Dad, and his oldest son Therry, *called* on her and Mom! Shucks, Aunt Madie thought that two white men were calling on them, as Dad and Therry were very fair, almost looking white. My Mom was very beautiful and dark skinned, with long hair and a thin figure. They were instantly attracted to each other, fell in love and married.

Dad was a big man with hazel eyes and close cropped hair, if any at all. He mostly shaved his head. He had a great laugh that I swore could rouse the dead. He loved his family and people. He was a hard worker and had many different jobs to provide for his family. Mostly he was a railroad worker and farmer. To quote my Dad, *"Any work is good. If it is honest it is good."*

Dad was born in 1881 in Tennessee and he was the only child of Curtis Eli Rucker and Emma (Goodman) Rucker, but he had a much younger half-sister. It was hard for me to believe that he would go on to have twelve children of his own. Actually, there were thirteen of us, as one died at birth. My Dad was married twice, once to the Mother of my two half-brothers and two half-sisters, and then to my Mother, Demore, who had nine of his children.

Curtis "Kirk" Rucker...

I deeply loved my Dad, and looked up to him. He was my *everything*. I especially loved our long walks as he would take me to the bus and pick me up at the bus stop every day. Early in the morning, we would walk and talk along the unpaved road. We would stop and eat from the fruit and pecan trees. As the warm breezes filtered through the deep cool shade of those beautiful trees, we were refreshed with scents of apples and wild berries, ripe grapes and pecans as well as the wild flowers along the roadside. It never failed, that by the time we reached the bus stop he was in the middle of telling me some fantastic thing that caused him to erupt with laughter. And when I was coming home I could hear that laugh—that howling laugh—before the bus even reached my stop. How it would embarrass me. I heard myself saying: "Gosh, why does my Dad have to laugh so loud and why does he look like my Granddad?" He would further embarrass me by what he wore; overalls with suspenders! Now these memories are so tender to me and I wonder why those things embarrassed me so much.

My Mother, Demore, was one of four children and she was very young when she met Dad. She had lost a sister at birth from epileptic seizures and she herself had started having them around her 12th or 13th birthday. I don't ever remember my Mom being able to talk to me or care for me or my brothers. She gave birth to nine children, and by the time I came along she was already very affected by the seizures. Dad tried everything to get her well and no good came of it. He never would put her "away," as they would say. He loved her and cared for her and taught us to care for her; and we loved her, too. She was my Mom. That is all that I actually remember about her, but I was told that she could sew really good, that she was a good cook, and that she loved to go dancing. (That explains why I love to cook and dance, but sewing, no! I can't even put in a hem! What's up with that?)

From the time of my birth, my brothers, Willie, R.D. and Lucky Time, and I were the only children still living at home.

We lived in the farming/ranch community of Newport, Arkansas, just 90 miles north of Little Rock. Our house sat in the center of a pasture where cows grazed all around us. It was very small, one bedroom, with no bathroom and no electricity, and of course, that meant no TV or radio. But it was my home, and I loved it! Looking out of my front door I could see my half-brother Therry's house to my right and to my left—about 6-12 blocks—was my friend Mable Brown's home.

Our *outhouse*—like everyone else's—was unforgettable and gross! I could never use it after dark because I was scared of the snakes and the weird sounds. So I would hold myself until daylight, or get one of my brothers to go outside with me and just go on the ground. I made them promise not to look.

There was always hustling and bustling going on around our house—cows, horses, chickens *talking* back and forth to each other. These animals were not ours, but belonged to the landowner. One of my grown brothers, **Curtis, Joe Nathan** (*Hot* as we called him)—was their foreman and one of my favorite things to do was watch him break the wild horses. *Hot* was a handsome young man, muscular, funny and had a wonderful gift-of-gab. He never met a stranger!

The barn was also a fun place to be when *Hot* brought the cows and horses in to feed them. My friend Mable and I would sit on the fence railing so we'd be out of his way, and get a good view of things. But I could only go there when my chores were done, and I had a LOT of chores. With no indoor plumbing, I would have to pump the water into pails and carry it inside for our cooking and washing. I'd do the laundry by hand, using a scrub board, and hang the clothes to dry on the clothes line that we had made. Plus, there was always the house to sweep out. Shucks! I would get up early and make my little brothers help me. Then we would clean ourselves up and head to the barn! What fun we had, and it was great to be free and be with my brothers and laugh...and *laugh...and laugh.*

We kept all our meats in a smokehouse—mostly wild meat—such as possums, rabbits, conies (badgers), and a little beef or pork on occasions. Oh, yes, we had fish from the pond at the back of our house, too, and we had a few chickens.

Sometimes we would go to Miss DeLottie's house for lunch, and boy she could really cook. She and her husband— Mr. Jeffro, the head foreman—lived in the big white house on the hill...above the barn. I sure miss her cookin' and all the fuss she would make over us kids. She always had a big smile, welcome arms, and open doors to us. Plus, she would allow me to go through her corn patch and pick fresh corn to take home.

SUNDAYS...

These were my very special days for *eating* because I would have chicken at my Grandmother Florence's home. She lived about thirty walking-minutes from our house and my brothers, Willie, RD, and I would linger along the way to pick from all the fruit trees and pecan trees and pick berries, nuts, and wild grapes. When we arrived we were almost full, but not too full for our Grandmother's good cooking. Grandmother Florence was a very special person in my life—like a *Mom* to me—and she made everything special for us. Even though Grandmother was in her late 70's—her skin rough and dry, her hands hard from farming and raising children—the love she gave us provided many tender memories. As she began those Sunday dinners, she would ask us to pick fresh strawberries, or kill a chicken, or pull fresh vegetables from her garden, but we didn't mind because we had fun doing it and loved her cooking.

Of course, we always went to Church first. As soon as we arrived at her house, off we would go! Wow! What great preachin' and singin' we heard! The Church was a great place, even though it was small and the only fresh air came from the open windows. Heck. Some Sundays in the summertime I could hardly keep awake because of the heat.

The women would dress in their Sunday *best* and the men, too. Well, I guess I did, too. I didn't have too many dresses, but Grandmother handmade me a couple just for Church—little flower dresses made out of grain and flour sacks. She would laundry them and make a wonderful looking dress just for me. Next thing I knew I looked like a regular girl instead of my usual *tomboy* look. After all, I had to be tough to oversee those adventurous brothers of mine, plus keep up with our active life in the fields.

Grandmother must have been important to the Church. They put our name on the building as Church Founders. Yes, my name is listed with my Grandmother Florence's, on the *Pilgrim Rest AME Church* in Post Oak, Arkansas.

When Sunday nights drew near it was always difficult for us to leave her, but we would start out for home and get ready for a full day of work and school again.

BY THE TIME I WAS TWELVE, my Dad started feeling poorly, and went to the hospital. He stayed for a long time, and I remember my bother, Joe Nathan, looking in on us—Mother, my little brothers and me—and making sure we had enough to eat. He would ride by every day and check on us. Then came the day that we learned Dad had died. At his funeral, folks spoke well of him:

> *"Mr. Kirk, as we all called him, had a joke and a smile for everybody. The joke could be on him or you, it made no difference—he got much joy and laughter. He liked to talk about his travel by steamboat and many construction jobs he worked on. He was fair and honest to deal with and only wanted what belonged to him. He didn't mind working hard...we will miss hearing him holler as he would near our homes. He always stopped to ask about each one in a friendly manner and joked about our gardens, fowls and flowers. He could have been called Jolly Kirk because he was that way all the time. He met no stranger...and if he heard someone speak of a need, and he possessed something that would help them, he would often bring it to them. May we long remember and cherish the smiles and sunshine he brought us."*

My life—really all of my family's lives—turned in new directions from that point to this.

Grandmother Florence, together with my older brothers, and sisters, made the difficult decision to place my Mother in a mental institution. At that time, there was no real understanding of how epilepsy effected people's mental abilities, and because my Mother could not (or would not) speak, there was no place for her in a regular hospital. By the time I became an adult I was extremely angered by those circumstances. Yet, I know now, that I had no control over them. Mother never recovered; she only got worse. They pulled all her teeth, gave her electric shock therapy, and tied her down for days. Every time I would hear about what was happening to her, I would cry and cry, and ask God, "Why?"

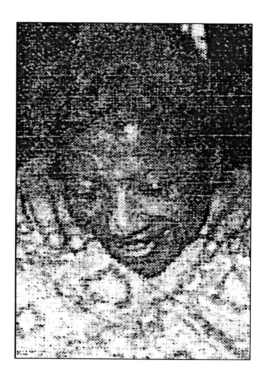

This photo of my Mother was taken in happier times— many years later when she was living in a nursing home and well cared for.

My youngest brother, LuckyTime, went to live with Grandmother Florence, even though she was in her late 70s. RD, and Willie went to JoNathan's home, and I came with my sister, Diane to Denver, Colorado. The family—or at least our family household of Dad, Mother, me and the little boys—was gone forever.

Lessons Learned...

From my Dad, Curtis "Kirk" Rucker, I received his deep work ethic, and the foundation of family responsibility. He showed me that these character traits were meant to be used in caring for our family—and others—that being a caregiver was a good thing. He taught me that if I wanted something, I had to work for it, whether it was doing household chores or working in the cotton fields. Now, hard work comes naturally to me—maybe too naturally.

From my Mother, Demore Tidwell Rucker: Even though you were unable to speak, your gentle heart, and quiet spirit never showed anger. Through your eyes, you showed me an attitude of love—and attitude of hope that I will always carry with me.

From my Grandmother Florence I learned that there is time to work, time to have fun, time for family and church. She had learned how to make *on-purpose* choices—conscious choices to stop the daily chores and "smell the babies."

Sent To Denver
By Way Of St. Louis, Missouri

My neighborhood park—28th Avenue & Gilpin

My *life* was forever changed. All I knew was my Dad had died and I hadn't even gotten to say *goodbye*. Everything I knew was lost to me. My home was empty—my family sad and separated—and no one would tell me about my Mother. I felt abandoned and alone—totally alone. WHY had all this happened to ME?

There was a small piece of me that was almost happy for my little brothers—especially Willie and RD who went to live with my most favorite brother, *Hot* (Joe Nathan). And even though I was pretty mad at Grandmother Florence, I knew that she carried a mighty love for baby Lucky-Time and would take good care of him. Growing up right there in our Arkansas farm country would have been my choice, too, but that wasn't what everybody else thought "best."

My older sister, Diane, had come home for Dad's funeral, and would be taking me back with her—to Denver, Colorado. As far as I was concerned, Colorado sounded like another planet. I wanted to scream, "I'M NOT GOING ANYWHERE!" But, I didn't say anything.

Diane was married, and had children of her own. It was decided that I would "fit right in." But money was tight. I sure didn't have any, and no one in Arkansas had any to send with me. So, Diane decided that we would stop in St. Louis, Missouri and visit our half-sister, Elva, and "see about" getting a little financial help. I had heard a lot about Elva from my Dad, as he often went to see her in St. Louis, but I personally didn't know her.

When we arrived at the hotel—which was Elva's home and business—Diane was invited right in, but I was directed to the back entrance. Back entrance? Why?

Well our visit was a short one, and the next thing I knew my sister, Diane, and I were in Denver. When I arrived at Diane's home, I was met by my brother-in-law, Lucious Cunningham. He welcomed me from that first moment, and made me part of his family. He had even made a private *nest* for me in their basement—my very own room. It was great! I fixed it up with my own favorite things. It wasn't long before I was interested in *American Bandstand* and had a poster of their dancers on my walls. I loved dancing and wanted to be on the show. But heck! I didn't even know where Philadelphia was!

Yes, my room in the Cunningham home was private, secure, and *my own*. It gave me just the comfort I needed to begin healing. Being separated from everything I had ever known or was familiar with was very emotionally ripping for me. I felt unwanted by my loving Grandmother, wondering why she wouldn't take me (although now I clearly understand why a woman in her late 70's could only handle one child). I also worried about what would happen to my brothers and my Mother, and still could not really believe that my Dad was gone.

Just after I arrived in Denver, my sister told me that a "nice girl lives in the house right back of us." She was so right! It wasn't long before I met my dear-friend-for-life, Alvesa. I always called her "Al." She was kind, sweet, and she taught me all about who to hang out with and who not to hang with. Al seemed to know everyone at school. We would often spend time together at the creamery on 34th, talk, eat hamburgers and play the juke box until we had no more money. What great fun we had, and we've remained friends all these years even though Al moved to Nebraska.

I soon met another friend, Eleanor, who lived right across the street from my house. She was tall, slender and smart, and I loved being with her. Eleanor lived with her Grandmother and they went to a Catholic Church where only Spanish was spoken. Sometimes I went to church with them and didn't understand a thing, but I didn't care, because I loved hanging out with my friend. (I still went to church with my family, too—Zion Baptist Church. We had the best pastor—Reverend Wendell T. Liggins—but during my teens

I didn't feel like I fit in.) Eleanor and I even dreamed of becoming *nuns!* I wonder if she ever did.

When I entered Baker Junior High, someone met me at the door and asked if I was in the right school. I said, "Yes, if this is Baker Junior High." It was, so I went to register and find my way around with my new friend, Eleanor, who went there, too! Baker was mostly Hispanic and I loved the kids, but they were sure different from the Mexicans I knew from Arkansas—who couldn't speak English and would be on the back of pickup trucks with me on the way to the cotton fields. These kids at Baker were *hip*, fun and I loved them!

Baker was a place where I fit in and even ran for Miss Teenage America and tried out for Chuck Wagon Entertainer, but I couldn't sing. So I decided to mime words to one of my favorite songs, enjoying being involved and having friends. After all, I made friends easily and even had a crush on Elvis, one of the most handsome boys at school. I remember in my heart, making up my mind that I would go steady with him. Elvis had an eye for many girls, but I knew that I would get him. Well that never happened! I did get him to come to my 16th birthday party and that was very exciting—Elvis at my party! Wow! Wow!

Moving up to East High School was great! I loved it from the very first day—as I woke early to prepare for the long walk across City Park to <u>my</u> school—some mornings just before the sun came up! At the beginning of the school years, when there was still enough early morning light, I would see golfers gathering to tee-off and I would have to dodge the balls. I made sure to stay well away from the golfers! As I walked, I met many friends and all of us—maybe five or six—would meet up at our park destination and talk and laugh all the way to school. Then we would do the same thing on the way home.

I recall a couple of bad times when bad men would want to try and trap me into their cars. Once, on the way to school, I had to pass by a smaller neighborhood park about 4-5 blocks from my home and it was a cold morning. I was walking fast, hurrying to get to school. I noticed a parked car with the hood up in front of the park, a man was standing outside of it. I was cautious and thought I should go across the street. Then I reasoned, no, I didn't want him to think I was afraid. So I picked up my pace and as I neared his car, he pulled out his penis and flashed it to me! I was so afraid! But I just kept walking faster and faster and I prayed, "Dear Lord, help me to get away from this horrible man!" Well, I made it to a busier street, where there were a lot of cars, and I waited near a person's home to see if that mad man would follow me. Thank God, he didn't. Boy was I scared and when I had to walk that way again the next day, I thought, this time if I see his car, I would go another way.

Well, I survived that! There were several other occasions when men tried to lure me into their cars by asking directions and then trying to grab me. Thank God that I was with friends. One other time, I'd gotten off the bus about two blocks from my turn off to go home, when I noticed I was being followed—by a car. I said, "No, I can't be followed." But, yes, I was. The car passed me three times, then came around the block again and slowed down right in front of me. I ran to a person's home and pressed their doorbell in alarm. My heart was beating so fast, surely they wouldn't follow me up to this home. Well, I wasn't sure. So I rang the doorbell again, and the people never came to help me. I knew that the people who lived here were older people, because I'd seen them working in their yard. I was so thankful that the bad men left! As I lingered on the front porch for 2-5 minutes, I was so thankful that I was safe, but puzzled why no one came to help me. Couldn't they see I was frightened and crying! Well, I thanked God for having a home there that I could run up to, and I forgave the couple for just standing by inside. I will never know what made the bad men go, but they went! Praise God!

Now, I loved my teachers at East High—all of them—but especially my math teacher, Mr. James, who was my only African American teacher. I remember him saying: "Polly, all you will need is good, basic math and you can run your own business." Mr. James, you were right! Many times when I was doing payroll or paying commissions, I have used what you taught me.

My PE teacher was great, too. I wanted to be like her and Mr. James, as they really showed that they cared for me, as well as others, by giving extra time and encouragement.

East High was primarily a well-to-do white school at the time I was there in the early sixties. So very few blacks were in any leadership position; only one, Walt Oliver, was elected our first Head Boy. Oh, yes, we could call him Head "Boy" back then without being degrading. We also had a Head Girl and she was beautiful and very friendly—Mona. I tried out to be the first black on the cheerleading team, but I had a couple of problems/concerns. One, I couldn't do the splits, and two, my grades were barely C's, so my PE teacher said, "Polly, you need to study first and bring your grades up." Shucks! I didn't like homework! But I would try and do it anyway. All I wanted to do was be a cheerleader, an actress in the drama club, fit in with the leadership group and graduate.

Was I crazy? Not only was I just a C-student, I also thought I could run for the Student Council! Well I did, but that didn't work out, and I finally found my own group—the Want-to-Be's. We hung out together, whined about the "pretty people" and their cars, and wished we could go skiing, too. But I loved my group. They were *real,* loving and caring, and I didn't have to try to fit in, I just did. We even had our own side of the lunchroom—the *Cool* side.

While at East, I also had the best looking Principal, Mr. Caldwell. WOW! So many of us girls had a crush on him.

I would wait outside the front door just to see him and Mr. James, until one day when Mr. Caldwell introduced me to his beautiful wife. So there went my crush! Funny how closely related crushes on teachers are, to finally discovering the role models they actually were in our lives.

These were also the days when everyone was infatuated with *movie stars*. Diahann Carroll was a role model for me because I really wanted to *look* like her. She was so beautiful and elegant, and spoke so well. Sidney Poitier was another role model who I just knew I would have dinner with someday. He showed me a manly style of elegance, was charming and very good looking, as well as a great actor and business man.

Well, I graduated! Just by the hair on my head—but I made it! Class of '63! I was so happy—out of school, and ready for life!

Lessons Learned...

Bad experience can be turned into something good, and we have to take our focus OFF of the bad stuff. The very thing that I'd always wanted to do—even as a small child—was to leave Arkansas and go to a *city*. Of course, I didn't want to go the way I went, with all the losses of relationships and separations. Yet, through those hard times—and through the ups and downs of my adolescent years—I was going to find a new beginning, and my destiny.

Without going through the bad, I would not have been able to go to the other side—new city, family, friends, experiences and new life. We must focus on the GOOD. There is always good, even when it is hard to see. LOOK FOR THE GOOD! LOOK FOR IT! It is there—LOOK!

From Flight Attendant
To Beauty College—Hair Stylist
(HOW I GOT INTO THE HAIR BUSINESS)

Toward the end of my Senior year at East High School, my counselor, Mr. Race, called me to his office. I thought, "What did I do wrong, now?"

WOW! To my surprise, he said, "Polly, I have worked out plans for all my students, but you."

"Don't worry, Mr. Race," I said. "I know exactly what I'm going to do; I'm going to be an actress!"

"Fine. Tell me the names of the plays and what part you played."

"Well...I played a character in *Keystone Cop* and in *Oklahoma,* and backup girl in *Chorus Line.*"

He just looked at me—as if I was dreaming. "Polly, I received this application on my desk today, and I was thinking about you."

"Me?"

"Yes, you. It's for a scholarship at the Cosmetology school."

"What's that, Mr. Race?"

"That's a hairdressing school."

"Oh! NO! I'm not going to be a hairdresser!"

"Why not? You can do your own hair very well. I've noticed how many different ways you wear your own hair. If not a hairdresser, then what else do you want to do, Polly?"

"Well, if I can't be an actress, then I'll be a Flight Attendant."

"Okay. Go and interview with the airlines; find out what the requirements are and get back to me."

Off I went to the airlines, and within minutes the interviewers told me that I was too short and my teeth were bad. "You could fix your teeth. However, if we did hire you, you'd have to move to Chicago. Our airlines base all of our *Negro* employees out of Chicago." That was my first negative employment experience—learning that companies in 1963-Denver were not as open to "negro" employees.

Civil Rights in Colorado in the 1960s was unique. Many *firsts* were happening in the local Black community. Governor John Love appointed Reverend Milton E. Proby from Colorado Springs to lead the first state Civil Rights Commission. East High School—approximately 90% white—elected their first black Head Boy. Neighborhoods were designated by nationalities: White, Black, Hispanic, Italian, Jewish...and unlike in the deep South, where prejudice was openly lived and expressed, Colorado Blacks learned to cope with the subtle, covert actions of non-blacks.

So, I went back to school and talked with Mr. Race again. He assured me that I would be a great hairdresser, and he showed me a scholarship from *Hollywood Beauty College.* They were looking for *African American—Negro—students!* Mr. Race added, "Polly, if at some time in your future you do decide to go to Junior College, you will have a way to support yourself." So we sat down and filled out the paper-work together.

A couple of weeks later, Mr. Race called me back into the office with the good news. "Polly, you've been accepted!" WOW! With graduation just a few weeks away, I now felt happy about my future. I thought about my Dad, and how hard he'd worked, and promised myself right then and there that I'd make him proud. I'd work hard, too, and become the best hairdresser in Denver...in all of Colorado!

Now, let me tell you about my first day at the *Hollywood Beauty College*! I was surprised at every turn that day! To start things off, I was late; I found the address—the building—but could not find the college. I finally discovered that it was on the garden level, and I'd been looking on the street level. No one had said anything about a *garden level*. A little out-of-breath, I walked through the doors and intro-duced myself. "I'm Polly Rucker, and I'm here for school." Well, by the startled look on the receptionist's face I knew she was unprepared to see me. With a quick "Excuse me, just a minute," she hurried to a back room, then out came she with a man following close behind her. As they walked toward me, I could see their reflection in the hall mirrors on the wall. They were both talking very fast. I quickly learned that the man was the director of the school.

"Welcome, Miss Rucker. My name is Mr. Harry Lardano, and I'd be happy to escort you to your classroom."

When I entered, the whole class quit talking. It was so very quiet. *What's the problem?* I thought. *Weren't they expecting a black girl? After all, they sent out scholarships for black students.*

After that organization meeting, Harry took me aside and said, "Polly, we will make no difference in you or for you. You will be treated the same as all the other students." That was somewhat reassuring until it came time to get a facial and makeup by one of the students. All we had in the school was makeup for <u>white</u> skin. Yes, we were being taught makeup techniques, and I had to participate!

Then, that same day, we were off to the Perm Class, and one of the students tried to *relax* my hair with regular perm solution. Well, after all of that I saw myself as I passed in the hall next to those mirrors. "Yikes! What in the world happened to me?" I looked like a black *Cousin It* (from the TV show the *Munsters*)! My hair was sticking out and it was curly, hanging to my shoulders and my face and neck were now powdered WHITE! I had to wear this all day long, and go home ON THE BUS this way. As Harry had said, he and his staff made no special exceptions between any of the students.

After a very interesting bus-ride—being the center of attention—I arrived home. My family said, "What in the world happened to you?"

With exhaustion in my voice, I answered, "My first day at Beauty School."

After that episode, I grew to love Beauty College, and especially one of my instructors, Mrs. Rose. She taught me a lot and she was very taken with me. I sometimes wonder if I wasn't the first "colored girl" she'd truly gotten to know, but if that were the case, she never told me or showed any prejudice. I loved her; she was beautiful and a great instructor. Mrs. Rose truly cared about each of her students.

I was so excited the day I graduated from *the Back-Room* where we worked on manikins and each other. I don't think that any of us thought we were ready for a *real* person, but it was time to do it. We went by numbers then, and not by first names. My number was #77.

So, that morning I arrived early and cleaned my station, did my own hair and makeup and I was ready. When the receptionist called #77 to the front, someone said, "That's you, Polly." Oh, yea! So I rushed to the front and introduced myself to the customer as #77.

The lady said, "I don't want a colored lady to do my hair. I want a white lady."

Now that I recall these times, I realize that I'd been in a sort-of equality bubble at the school. But, when that lady refused my service, I was faced with the *color* issue. She didn't care about my ability, only the shade of my skin.

Well, Harry came out and said, "What's the problem?" The lady repeated herself...that she only wanted a white woman to do her hair. And Harry said to her, "You either have #77 do your hair, or no one here will do you hair." Once again, Harry stood by his word that I would be treated equally.

IN THE ENTRY LEVEL of my career, I ran into this type of prejudice often. Women would come in to the salons and find out that I was black; they would make some excuse to step outside; and I would not see them again. This went on through the 60s and into the 70s in Denver. By the 80s, white women seemed to be okay with me being black—as long as I could do their hair *good*, and I could! I continued to improve my techniques and skills, and was becoming not just a good hairdresser, but an excellent hair-stylist! Now my clientele is largely white and we develop good friendship-relationships.

I was on a one-year plan to graduate even though it was a 9-month course, because of my full scholarship. However, when I found out I was pregnant (and got married) I took a sabbatical to have my son, Bryan, and ended up with more time off than I had asked for due to my *new mother's* heart-change. I was totally in love with my new baby boy. After seeing, holding and caring for him, I just couldn't leave him right away, so I took six months off and lost a few credit hours. Upon re-entering school I had to make up approximately 300 lost hours.

It worked out okay. When I went back I had new classmates and developed new friendships. I finished well, and graduated in 1965. Harry was very proud of me—as I was.

By this time I was up to my ears juggling all the parts of my life: still learning to be a wife and mom, and now looking for a job. I am so thankful for the good help of Bryan's grandmother. What a lifesaver to have her in my life and Rose, my friend, both taking turns caring for baby Bryan.

My friend, Rose, was someone I looked up to and envied. She seemed to have so many friends and boyfriends, and she was beautiful and fun! But one day I came home and she and my son's dad had been together (intimately) and I saw signs of lipstick on his mouth, and her hair was all out of shape. I knew right away they had been making-out. I was so hurt and mad! How could my best friend make love to my husband? How could he do this with her? HOW? Well, I kicked her out! When I asked him what happened, he said, "We never intended anything to happen. We just started fooling around and then kissing. But we never had sex." Well, that made me feel a little better, but here I was now, with no babysitter for the next day, and I was trying my hardest to believe my husband.

Rose and I were never close after that, as I had lost trust in her. But I did forgive her. We remained cordial, and I know in my heart she is sorry for what happened. I forgave my husband, too, not knowing all of the challenges he and I would face in the years to come.

Lessons Learned...

Prejudice *hurts*! That's not news to anybody until it happens to you. I suppose I felt some of the separateness in high school, but not so openly. I remembered my childhood in Arkansas, and how everyone—even the few whites I knew—treated all of us kids with kindness. Maybe the adults felt things differently, but I didn't remember it. I also discovered that a lot of very wonderful people—both black and white—had come across my path, and I was a better person because of their caring and compassion. That's the kind of person I wanted to be—colorblind.

I didn't realize it until much later that these were also days of learning how to forgive. Forgiveness has become so important in my life—accepting forgiveness, and extending forgiveness. I highly recommend it! It brings FREEDOM to both heart and soul!

Puppy Love, Pregnancy and Marriage

JAMES....

It was during this time—just as I graduated from high school, and began my classes at *Hollywood Beauty College*—that I met James.

He was tall and cute and had great sex appeal! WOW! I loved the way he looked from the first time I saw him lo-riding in his car on the streets in my neighborhood. One beautiful Sunday evening, as my friend Rose and I walked to the bowling alley, James slowly followed us in his car. He started talking to me and I told him that I couldn't—wouldn't—get in the car with him. So, he got out of the car and walked with us. We walked and talked...and walked and talked...to the bowling alley which was about 6-10 blocks. That very day, I noticed that he'd been drinking, but didn't think twice about it. I was so flattered that a handsome man would be interested in me! After we finished bowling, I felt safe enough to have him drive me home, where he politely walked me to my door. I allowed him to kiss me, and boy did I love that! I knew then that I wanted to see him more, and more I did. Finally we had sex and I got pregnant.

James knew that I was pregnant before I did and he wanted me to go to a doctor. But I said, NO! Pregnancy filled me with fear. How could I ever support a child? I was barely out of high school, and the little bit of money I had was tied up with the Beauty College tuition. I told myself that I didn't want any children because I'd raised children all of my life. And I told God that I was really mad at Him for allowing this to happen. "After all, God," I said, "my friend down the street messes around a lot and she's not pregnant! What's up with that God? Why me?" Now that I recall that silent conversation, I bet God was just shaking His head!

Well after 3-4 months of denial, and a visit to the therapy office at the baby clinic, I knew I had to have this child. But would I keep him? My sister, Diane, said, "Yes." She said, "Polly, you're not going to be the first person in our family to give up a baby."

James and his Grandparents wanted us to marry, too. After all, women (girls) in my day didn't just get pregnant— they married! So, at the age of 19, I married James Sanders.

We were married by Reverend Liggins at Zion Baptist Church and even though I was five months pregnant, I wore a beautiful layered white dress trying to hide my growing figure, but everyone could tell. The ceremony was brief. I know that the minister wasn't happy with us at all. However, my wonderful sister, Diane, gave us a great wedding reception! She worked so hard, cooking ham, roast beef, chicken with all the trimmings of potato salad, and greens. Everyone ate, laughed and had fun, including me, and that began my life with James and my soon-to-be-born son. It was a Sunday, and I was happy.

Well, we didn't go on a honeymoon, as we couldn't afford it. But I was so excited to start my new life with my new husband, and make our first house (apartment) into our *home,* that going away on a honeymoon didn't really matter to me. I was also still in beauty school, and didn't want to miss any classes.

I loved our little apartment on Marion Street. We were so happy there; it was close to my favorite Mexican restaurant which was just up the alley, and I could also walk to a small neighborhood grocery, the Laundromat and the bus line. I couldn't drive yet. Oh, I could have learned, but why learn when we only had one car and my husband needed that to get to work and it was too far to take the bus. So, I took the bus everywhere. It was great! I was young and full of energy and life, and I was happy. We also had our friends over to our home a lot, and I would cook and so would James. He fixed barbequed ribs and we would play cards and the party would be *on*, with great music in the background. I didn't know that we were poor then, because we were filled with laughter, joy and great friends (mostly my husband's friends and their wives), which I loved.

During this same time—of going to Beauty College, setting up our home, and getting used to the realities of being married—I was also definitely aware that I would soon be a Mom. I set my course to be the best Mother I could be. I read all the books on infant and child care-giving I could get my hands on, comparing my childhood memories of raising my little brothers with what the books said to do. I discovered that I was already well prepared to be a good Mother.

Bryan's arrival was HARD LABOR—14 hours—and a breach delivery. James stayed with us in the labor room and was so proud to have a son. Then, when the hospital nurse put that cute, sweet little baby in my arms I said to God and to the nurse, "Who couldn't love or want this baby? Who?" Well, that *who* had been me. But I fell in love with my son from that moment on, and I still have that same love for him today. Our hearts are truly bonded.

My son, Bryan...

Becoming Bryan's Mother was so wonderful! I loved it! He was such a beautiful baby, and I found that I adapted easily to this role, because I had already learned to handle so much responsibility. I finished Beauty College, and within a very short time after Bryan's birth, he and I were taking bus-rides in search of work. James was working hard, but if we wanted to have a home of our own someday, it would take two incomes to build any kind of savings account and a financially stable life together.

Lessons Learned...
Even though I felt afraid, the new life inside me gave me hope. Nothing can compare to the moment when my son reached out to me and took hold of my hand and my heart. I was very hope-filled! I remembered the example of my parents and their commitment to each other. James' grandparents also had a strong marriage relationship. And, now, I had my husband, my son, and an apartment that I fixed up. We were happy, and I just knew that I would get a *good* job! I was so full of *hope*...FULL!

MY FIRST JOB...

I circled job ads, made phone calls, and went to what seemed like hundreds of beauty salons. Most shop owners were not used to a black hairdresser applying to work in a white salon in the 60s, and I must admit that at that time I needed a little *finish* work in my appearance. Oh, I no longer looked like *Cousin It,* but I didn't have a *look* yet, either. I wore my long, curly hair up in a bun or twist, and I also wore to make me appear taller, as I was only five feet tall.

After looking and looking, I was finally hired by Miss Minnie, the owner of *Minnie's Salon* on the west side of Denver. "When can you start?" she asked. "Right now," I said, and boy was I ever happy. I could now prove to myself that I was a good hairdresser; I wanted to work and work hard I would! This salon was in a mostly Hispanic area of Denver, and I enjoyed working with my happy and energetic clients. However, in all the excitement of getting my first job, I'd forgotten how far away it was from my home. Six days a week I had to take THREE buses there and three buses home again. My husband never offered to help me with transportation, or to help me with our son. Thank Goodness for James' Grandmother who offered to watch Bryan, and to Aunt Juanitha who helped, too. Very early in the mornings, I would drop off Bryan at his Grandmother's and pick him up again long after the sun had set.

Now that I was a Mom, working full-time, and trying to keep up with things at our little apartment, I began to see life more seriously. However, my husband, James, still acted the teenager. I felt like I was being pulled in a hundred different directions, while he went off to *party.* I began wondering who he was partying with and resenting his lack of interest in our home, our son, and our marriage. I had always taken on a lot of responsibility and this was no different. But, I noticed that resentment set in and I wanted some things to change!

Well, after approximately one year I was let go—fired—
from Miss Minnie's because of having too many challenges.
Whether buses were running late, or the baby was fussy, or
I'd had a rough night at home, I still needed to be at work
on time. Clients didn't like waiting. I was just *sick* about
leaving. Miss Minnie had started giving me more tasks, and
I not only enjoyed them, but found that I could handle lots
of responsibility and could also *do* hair, and do it well. I was
working long, hard hours, while managing all the pieces of
my life. Traveling such a far distance from home was just
did not work.

I now decided that I had to get work closer to my home. I
couldn't drive yet. We still had only one car and my husband
needed it. He took me everywhere I wanted to go, or I would
take a bus, or call a friend. It wasn't so bad.

My job hunting efforts were discouraging to say the
least. With every "No thank you—not hiring," I had to overcome great feelings of rejection, doubt. Plus, at twenty years
of age, I looked only seventeen or eighteen, and everyone
thought I was too young to be a hairdresser.

But, one day, I said to myself, "I'm going to get up, get
dressed, go out and get a job!" So I did! I stopped at this
small, quaint, salon near City Park in Denver, near my son's
Grandmother's home, and said, "My name is Polly Sanders,
and I'm looking for a job as a hairdresser."

The woman barely glanced at me and said, "We don't
need a hairdresser."

Just as I turned to go, this other hairdresser said, "Vera.
Remember, I'll be starting part-time soon, and you can't do
all the walk-in's and your clients, and mine too."

Vera said, "You're right, Martha." Then Vera said to me,
"Let me take a look at our calendar and see when you can
start work."

SO, there it was, an open door for me, and I took full
advantage. I worked hard, and Vera quickly liked my personal

skills with the women clients. It didn't take long before she began giving me more responsibility and hours. And best of all, this is where I met my *friend-for-life*, Martha!

The MARRIAGE...

I was trying every day to learn to re-trust my husband, my son's Dad, but our home life got progressively worse. So, when my sister, Elva—from St. Louis—came to visit Diane not too long after my beautiful Bryan was born I was happy that James was away at work.

Oh, yes, I remember that day! I knew that Diane was going to bring Elva to our little apartment, and I cleaned and cleaned, trying to make everything look great. I was very proud of our home! Bryan and I were waiting, and do you believe it, I *showed her around*! Shucks, it was only a one bedroom apartment, but it was mine, and I loved it. I served tea and cookies, and darn, if a mouse didn't appear and run across the floor right at her feet! *Oh, no!* I thought. *Why does that little mouse have to come out now?* Well, Elva saw it, screamed, and said, "A mouse! Diane, let's go!" So off they went and I was left with my tea and my thoughts. *What must my sister think about me?* Oh, well. Nothing I could do about it. So, I cleaned again, cared for my son and got ready for my husband who was due home any minute.

Oh, yes, one of my biggest fears was that the mice would come and chew on my son as he slept. So I always had him sleep in our bedroom, next to my side of the bed. I woke up at the slightest sound, but thank God, no mouse ever touched sweet Bryan.

I continued to work long hours which became more and more of a way to escape being around my husband. But my desire to move to a better neighborhood also pushed me to earn more money. There was something inside me that *told* me that if we lived in a *nicer area* we'd be happier. So, eventually, to a better neighborhood we did move.

After three years in that first apartment, we found what felt like a BIG home. It was only a two bedroom apartment, but I had my first laundry room—no more carrying clothes to the Laundromat—and my first dining room, which was attached to the living room. Boy, I loved that place especially since it was only four blocks from my sister, Diane's home where I had been raised. Plus, it was close to Colorado Blvd. and the bus line. A nice little grocery store was close by and even a great big park, as well as my favorite chicken restaurant which was now within walking distance. We also had great neighbors—the Jackson's—whom I loved and they love me.

Mr. and Mrs. Jackson were our wonderful neighbors, and they would help me with Bryan after school. Because of my late salon hours, Bryan's Dad's long hours away from home, Bryan could have been left alone and hungry. But Mrs. Jackson would feed him and allow him to stay with her until I got home.

There were many times I would arrive home to *hell.* That's right, *HELL.* Even as I entered my door I could hear the loud music, and knew it would be a rough night. My husband had been "out with the guys," and when I walked in the door he was ready to argue, with cursing, and threats. His favorite thing to tell me was, "I'm gonna kick your ass." Our happy married life had turned into misery, and I was always terrified that James would hit me, hurt me and/or hurt our son, Bryan.

Daily life was not easy, but my son, Bryan, made all the difference. Once Bryan entered school, I arranged my work hours and became involved in my son's school and was even PTA president during his elementary and senior high school years. With my salon tips I bought Bryan the best clothes, and enrolled him in every class and lesson I could...from skiing to tennis to swimming and camps. I said, "Nothing is too good for my son." I was so focused on giving Bryan the things I never had, and trying to erase the bad things he'd experienced, that sometimes I went a bit overboard.

I remember one specific day when Bryan spoke up. "Mom, why should I take up skiing?"

I answered, "Why not?"

"Mom, none of the kids in my neighborhood can ski."

"Well, you can ski with other kids at school."

"Mom, I'm bused to school, and those kids don't hang with us."

"O.K., Bryan, you have a point." So, from that point on, I let him choose his own extracurricular activities—as long as it wasn't hanging out with bad groups or getting involved with drugs or sex.

LAST STRAW...

James, Bryan and I lived in our Madison Street apartment for almost seven years. For awhile, I thought that I was able to understand James, and I held on to many different threads of hope. I believed that my husband was seeking the love, acceptance and healing that he had never known as a child, yet so desperately needed, through drinking, drugs, and women. And, I automatically sought love and acceptance through approval, success and recognition. We made quite a pair. Both of us were so messed up from the lack of knowing love and acceptance in our <u>insides</u> that we tried to find it through wrong methods and wrong thinking.

One day, I came home from work, and Bryan said, "Mom, Dad threw me from the kitchen to the couch at the door." Instantly, I was enraged. Well, I grabbed-up my son and just held him, then told Bryan to run. "RUN to Aunt Diane's and don't look back no matter what. Just run, Bryan, run." Every fiber inside me was screaming...*If I don't leave James, he might kill my son!*

That's when I made up my mind that we would leave. I didn't know how we could do it, or where we would go, but

47

I knew that we had to leave. James was in the house, so my anger was driving me, and I started to make plans.

James was full of alcohol and drugs, and it was a rough time for me. Like many other nights he cursed me—slapped me against a wall—kicked me in my ass—then he fell asleep. Somehow I managed to keep my own anger in check, and once he was asleep I could almost see the hurts and pains that he was dealing with inside. I loved him so much, and tried with everything in my heart to turn our home life around. But now I felt like a failure—unable to change anything—and now he had turned on our son. I knew we HAD to leave. I pulled out a few of my clothes, so I'd have something to wear to work the next day, and ran. I ran and I ran, and I cried, and I cried; but I was free! I felt free. Even though I had no home, I felt free because I was free inside!

Well, after several days I returned to the apartment to get some clean clothes and I found my home in the worst mess you could ever imagine; there were blonde wig boxes in my living room and the white/pasty evidence of sexual activity in my bed AND my son's bed! This was all too much! I couldn't take it any longer. The hurt, anger and fear were all mixed up inside of me. I was overtaken with rage, and I knew that I was going to kill James when he came home. I found his gun—which he kept in his drawer—and I sat on my front porch waiting for him to arrive. I knew in my heart that he was dead!

When James got home I pointed that thing straight at him. "You son-of-a-bitch! You can't keep doing these things to us, James! You just can't."

"I will kill you! You hear! I will kill you," James screamed back at me.

Kill me? He was so high he didn't even know what he was saying. *Kill me*!

Our good neighbor, Mr. Jackson, heard the commotion and called the police. When they arrived they took James into a different room and talked with us separately. After hearing what had happened, and seeing the mess in the house, they asked—actually ordered—me to "Go."

"Why should I go, when he caused all the problems? He's the guilty one! I won't go. I'll kill him first," I screamed; I was so driven by anger and hurt and rage.

But they talked some sense into me and said, "Mrs. Sanders, if you were to kill your husband, your son would grow up an orphan, because you'd be in jail."

Well, right there I got hold of myself, thinking, *I don't care if I go to jail, but I don't want my son to be an orphan.* I put the gun down, grabbed-up a few of our things and off I walked to my sister's home a few blocks away.

Bryan and I only stayed with my sister for a few days, as she had her hands full with five children, her own a husband, and a few problems of their own. By now I knew that I'd done everything I could to keep my home intact. But no more! I had to get out to keep my son and me safe. I had to! I worked out an arrangement with a friend and stayed at her home until I was able to re-occupy my home. James and I separated, divorced. I got the apartment AND all the bills, and full custody of my son. James and I had endured this marriage for 10 years.

Lessons I Learned...

What I learned from this marriage is that you can love each other, but when two people are emotionally sick inside, no *things* or no *outside* emotional love can sort out unresolved inner issues. I had to admit that I could not "fix" my husband, or our marriage. I had to acknowledge the danger of being co-dependent, and protect my child and myself. However, I also felt the love and support of friends and family, and learned that when I didn't turn away from them, they were there for me—I was not alone. I had help but I had to ask for it and use wisdom in my decisions—my choices—not just my feelings.

Through It All
My Gifts and Talents Grow

When I think of these years in my life, I sometimes wonder if the daily tasks of my career weren't the heavy-duty *glue* that held me together, plus providing the finances for our survival.

I had been working with Vera and Martha now for almost three years. Martha and I had become very close. She was a great hair designer, mother, and a great friend. One day the salon was quiet and I said to Martha, "I think I'll go and look for us a larger salon to work in," and off I went.

I remembered this one salon I saw as I would go by it on the bus. They were always busy, and it would be much easier for me to get to from home. So, I decided that I would apply there. When I walked in and met the receptionist, an older woman who was somewhat warm, she said, "Wait a minute, and I will get Earl for you." As I waited, I sized up the salon and its workers. I saw an older clientele, but there was this young hairdresser there who seemed to be very busy and popular, and there were a few younger clients, too.

Well, Earl introduced himself to me and asked if I could talk with him in the back room.

"Sure," I said.

"Do you have a clientele that might follow you to a new salon? Then just tell me a little bit about yourself."

"I do have several clients that I know would follow me," I answered, with as much confidence as I could muster. "And, I feel like I've outgrown where I'm working at now. I'm looking to grow and move to a more progressive salon. *And*, if you hire me, you will need to make room for my friend Martha."

"Well, is she as pretty as you?"

"Prettier, and she is white."

"White?"

"Yes, I can do white hair too."

He seemed pleasantly surprised and gave both of us a job on the spot. "When can you start?"

Well, Martha and I gave notice to Vera, left there and began working for Earl. We were both very thankful for what we had learned in Vera's shop, yet even more excited for better days ahead.

Earl's Beauty Salon was the next stop on my career-building ladder, and it was just like Earl said, the clients would—and did—love me. However, the staff had a little harder time with accepting me as their equal. Oh, well! I served them and loved them and I *grew* on each of them. That *warm* woman at the desk turned out to be Earl's wife who helped me with many things, not only bookings, but with a greater understanding of my personal life, and how to handle things there. Great relationships grew out of this opportunity. Martha and I became even closer friends, and we both loved Earl and his wife and their two daughters.

Some time later, Martha came in to work one day, and decided that she had had enough of doing hair, so she quit. She then went to work at the phone company in Denver, and became a great sales person. A wonderful mother, grand-mother, and true friend, she still continues to support me with little encouraging notes, financial support for my Ministry, and much prayer.

Earl showed me such great favor. He saw a potential for leadership in me that I didn't see in myself, and took me to meetings at the *Board of Cosmetology*. He was a member, and through those meetings, and our discussions afterward, he taught me the rules of leadership and getting ahead. So with his help, I began to grow a belief in myself and the abilities that God had given me.

I was quick to learn, and off I went to work on the Board of Cosmetology, and was then elected to the office *President of the Denver and State Cosmetology Association*, and that really began my growth experience as a leader. When I look back on those times, I see that I had always been leading, whether it was in my home as a child—as head of the family from the age of 6 or 7—to leading and making decisions in my marital home, and the workplace.

Ties That BIND...

James and I had been divorced now for about one year but my heart was still tied to him. I still had such deep emotional (soul) ties to James. I knew that I still loved him, and believed that I only divorced him out of fear. So, one day, I went to his place of work downtown, and asked him to come and sit with me in my car. (Yes, I'd finally gotten a drivers license and car, and an extra job where I needed to use a car to make extra money.) I remember saying to James, "Do you still love me?"

"Yes," he *thought!* But he didn't know about re-marriage. "What would people say?"

I said, "The hell with people. We are re-marrying for our family!" I also made it clear that we both needed to get into counseling. He agreed, and we set a date.

So off we went to Las Vegas, had a fun wedding at a lovely little chapel surrounded by flowers, and we had a great time. It looked and felt like we were on our way to a mended relationship. When we got home, we started our counseling group right away. But, you've heard it before, I *should have known.* James only went a couple of times and quit. Within a very short time, I found myself back with the same issues—watching this man bring alcohol and drugs back into our house, and wondering which of his many "lady friends" he was with. Still, over the next five years I held on to a belief that a miracle would happen.

These were difficult days for my son, Bryan, too. I found myself praying that he would surround himself with the right friends. To me, that meant kids who went to school and didn't do drugs, and I do believe that he had a lot of good friends. I knew most of them, and had a chance to meet their Mom's on occasion, either at school or when I voted at the polls, or when I would pick Bryan up, or they would pick their son or daughter up. I remember only one young man who had a drinking problem. I loved him, had a lot of compassion for him and prayed for him. I now wonder where he is and how he is doing.

Finally, I'd had enough. Our painful marriage relationship had worn me down and I couldn't go on. James and I were both unhealthy emotionally and both of us needed something that we couldn't find or give to each other. So we divorced again and I was left with all the debt. It was very hard for me financially and emotionally; I felt like I had failed. But, if nothing else, I am a survivor. I continued in counseling and it helped me to understand myself more and discover why I chose the men I did.

Years later I was able to truly and deeply forgive James. I could look at his (our) lives and see how a lack of love throughout a family's history can create a very destructive cycle. James' parents had given him up at the age of a year and a half, and he went to live with his grandparents who didn't hold him or show him any emotional affection. They were afraid to show the emotional love of holding and kissing, thinking it would *make* him too feminine. So they withheld physical and emotional love, the very thing he needed—the very thing I needed and our son needed.

Second-time-around Lesson Learned...

I know now that James and I were not each other's *answer*. We both carried tremendous *voids* inside of us—rejection and abandonment, fear, loneliness, bitterness, blame, great pain and hurt, unfulfillment, resentment and not knowing love/care. What we truly wanted and needed could not be found in a person, or thing—money or success. It was time—way past time—for me to *dig* deep and search out answers elsewhere.

* * * * * * * *

Diving DEEP into my career...

Earl and his wife, Helen, became like surrogate parents to me, and their encouragement in my personal and professional life were *life-savers*. However, there came the day when I had to leave the *nest*. But I was ready. Earl had helped me *grow up* and planted all his years of experience into me. He had opened many doors for me. Now I was ready to sail, and I knew just where I wanted to land, a very prestigious place in Denver called, *Cherry Creek*. But who would hire me there?

One day I was at a Hair Stylist Conference sitting at the bar with other hairdressers. I was telling this male hairdresser named Phil that I wanted to work in *Cherry Creek*. "So, why don't you?" he said.

"Are you kidding, Phil? You know no one is hiring a black in *Cherry Creek*."

"I will!"

That's great, I thought, *and they aren't hiring Mexicans either.* Well, I left my phone number with him anyway, and out of the blue sky, Phil called me and asked if I still wanted to work in *Cherry Creek*. "Are you kidding? Of course I do!"

But how could I leave Earl after all he has done for me? HOW? I gave it a lot of thought and I asked God to help me. Then, I asked for a meeting with Earl after work and explained how much he had helped me and how he had caused me to grow and now I was going to move to the *Cherry Creek* salon of *Antoine Du Chez*. I asked Earl to release me, and he did—with his blessings upon my life and family. Well, I cried and cried, and I wondered how I would make it without Earl and [wife] in my life every day. They had been there for me for over seven years.

The new salon was exciting, but scary! I remember saying to myself that I wasn't going to let my insecurities keep me from this wonderful door that had opened for me. Thank God I had a good clientele and for the most part they followed me to the new salon.

Then, one day, Phil got another partner—Michael Taylor—and everything changed. In the end, the changes were for the better, but WOW, I had to learn to let go of *everything* I knew about hair and do it HIS way. Michael was well established in Denver and his name carried a lot of weight. But boy was it hard to change my way of doing things. However, I did, and what I learned gave me greater skills, and the newer techniques that have helped me attract more business clientele.

The greatest challenge for me came when he asked me to be his *assistant* which meant that I had to give up control. I must have really wanted that position and I learned then just what a strong-willed person I was—and that I had persistence. I didn't give up even when I felt like it, because in my heart I knew that I belonged there. I wanted to work in *Cherry Creek* and now I was there and I wouldn't let my ego and pride keep me from succeeding.

Well, I quickly found out that by letting go of my fears and insecurities, I was able to greatly improve customer relationships and my skills in cutting hair. Looking beyond where I was to where I wanted to be in this industry and in my life, I discovered that I could work with Michael and allow his experience help me get where I wanted to be. And, there it did! Whoever would have believed that I would go to New York, Paris and England? Whoever thought that this little girl from the fields of Arkansas would ever go to these great places? Well, by becoming Michael's assistant, I was able to travel with my boss and he opened many, many doors for me and many great opportunities. Michael helped me—encouraged me—to run for President of the *Colorado Hairdressers and Cosmetology Association*. I did and I won! Eventually I went into partnership with Antoine Du Chez.

* * * * * * * *

WELL, here we are the highlights of my career so far. I'm now 63 years young and I'm still doing hair 10-12 hours a day in my salon in *Cherry Creek*. I love my relationships with my co-workers and my clients: our long chats, some debates, lots of laughter, and sometimes crying together. All-in-all, I was made for *doing* hair and hair was made for me to *do*. *Thank you*, to all the people in my life who saw that I had a gift for hair-styling and helping people, and encouraged me to move beyond life's heartbreaks and setbacks.

CAREER BENCHMARKS:

1. 1973 ✺ Won the *Madam C.J.Walker Award* for outstanding achievements in hair industry.
2. 1973-83 ✺ Became the Platform Educator for *Revlon* and *Redken* and traveled to many states...places I would never have gone to without this position.
3. 1974 ✺ My travels to France and England with my boss, Michael Taylor, for the world championship competition in hairstyling. WOW!
4. 1978-79 ✺ The first time my boss came to me and said I had hit my goal of $80. WOW! I couldn't believe it!
5. 1980-84 ✺ Won the position of President of the <u>State Hairdressers Association</u>.
6. 1984 ✺ My dream come true—opening of my own salon in fashionable *Cherry Creek*.
7. 1995 ✺ At the age of 50, I was the featured model on the front cover of the Fashion section of the *Denver Post* newspaper.
8. 2005 ✺ My dream fulfilled again—opening of my own salon in central *Cherry Creek*.

PLUS ð Ongoing Ministry television interviews with various celebrities such as my Salon client Bertha Lynn (TV Anchor).

Lessons Learned...

The discovery of my natural talents and abilities has given me some of the most pleasurable moments of my life. This is one area of my life that seemed to flourish even when I thought I was struggling. It is a true blessing to be able to *work* in a job or career that I LOVE! I love doing hair, helping people and the service industry. The very things I always needed—hugs and cherished relationships—are there every day in my work. Every time I do someone's hair, I greet them with a hug and close our time together with, "I love you," and they hug and love me, too. What a great job! And I even get paid to do it!

Family Support...

My Sister, Diane...

Diane is my oldest full-sister.
By the time I was ten, Diane moved away from home. She came back to Arkansas often, and seemed like a movie star to me, driving up in a big car and bringing gifts. She brought a smile to everyone, especially Dad, telling us about her life in Denver and her family. How thankful I am for her! After my Dad's death and my Mother was moved into a mental institution, Diane was there for me. She seemed to intuitively understand my feelings of abandonment and did all she could to love me unconditionally, and care for all my material needs. She brought me to her home in Denver, gave me my own room in her beautiful house, and *raised* me with great care. It was hard for me to *mind* her at first. I was a rather strong-willed child and I had to learn to obey her, which I did, after she and I had several *discussions* at the top of our lungs. Like my own Mother might have done I felt like Diane wanted to keep me a *little girl* always wearing those pretty tie-back dresses. But she also knew how important friendships are and she helped me discover new friends in the neighborhood. I know now, that God placed her in my life to help me become ALL that He has for me. Diane reached

out to me and helped me through many difficult challenges in my life. Thank you, Diane, for all your nights of crying out to God for me, hoping that I'd turn out okay. Thank you for showing me that God can take what seems bad and turn it into *good*. You are the very best sister—and friend—a person could have. I love you and I'm very thankful for you!

My Brother, RD...Dr. R.D.Rucker, LLD

Five and one-half years younger than me, RD became the scholar of our family. His deep passion for learning not only inspired us—his family—but every person he met. RD received his law degree from the University of Texas School of Law and was admitted to the Texas Bar in 1985. His careers included: public defender, prosecutor, assistant Texas Attorney General, and college professor of Russian history, as well as authoring several books.

RD and I became very close in our adult years, and he encouraged me to write this book. "Polly, "he said, "Go forth and do what your call and purpose is. Share your story and encourage all those you meet so that they, too, can overcome great adversities and hurts in their lives. Show them that God loves them and that He has a plan to help them overcome all the woundedness, pain, rejection, fear and abandonments issues in their lives."

Dr. R.D. Rucker passed on to Eternal Life August 13, 2003.

Yes, Dr. Rucker, I have come to the place of writing this book, and I am so thankful for you and your great love and all the care you had for me. We enjoyed many special times together. Your spirit is always alive in me and I WILL share my story with all I meet, knowing that you are proud of me—as I've always been proud of you.

My Sister, Elva...

Elva was my oldest sister (half-sister). We had the same Dad, but different Mom's. I will share a bit more detail about this relationship, as it demonstrates how God continually works with us and within our relationships with each other.

I didn't know much about her when I was younger, only that she was married to a Jewish man and owned a hotel business in St. Louis, Missouri...and that she often passed as white. After I'd lived in Denver for awhile I heard that she'd hidden some of our family, who dropped by unexpectedly, from her white friends. That made me remember the way she'd acted when Diane and I came through town, and Elva made me enter the hotel from the back, where the workers entered. Just thinking about it made me feel like I was her servant—not her sister.

However, all of my life Elva, sent me Christmas cards, but they only had her name **stamped** in the card, nothing personal was ever written in them. So every year I would read it and tear it up! I just *knew* that she didn't like me or want to have a relationship with me; this hurt me very much and added to the emotional pain I was experiencing in daily life.

When I was about 27-28 years old, I made a trip back to St. Louis just to talk with Elva. I felt that I'd carried the brokenness of our relationship too long; I wanted some kind of resolution.

So when I called her—at her home which was in the hotel she owned—she said, "Girl, my air conditioner is down and it is mighty hot. You don't want to come to my house."

"Okay," I said. "Then meet me somewhere, so that we can talk." I just knew that there was something about *me* she didn't like, and her excuse to keep me from coming to her home just strengthened my feelings. What could it be about me that she didn't like? We'd never lived under the same roof, had not developed a relationship, or had any arguments.

Well, Elva said she'd meet me at a nice park-like area by the St. Louis River. The day was beautiful, sunshiny, and the park was not crowded with people. I told her a little bit about my working-life as a hairdresser, and she seemed pleased to hear that I was doing okay. Then I tried to get her to open up to me and talk about our Dad, asking her to share her memories.

"I know a lot about your Dad, but I'm not tellin' you."

When I asked "Why?" she wouldn't answer me, and within a few minutes our get-to-know-each-other conversation was over. I was left even more confused than before.

I remember thinking, *Dad, this is your favorite daughter?* Other family members had told me over the years that Elva and Dad were very close. *WOW!* I thought. *Dad, how could you love a hateful person like her even if she was your oldest daughter? HOW?* I left that place with even more anger, hurt and misunderstandings.

Well, before my brother, Dr. Rucker, died, he told me, "It isn't that Elva doesn't like you, Polly. She has a hard time *seeing you* and being with you because you look so much like your Mom. Elva just never understood why Dad left her mother, and then married our Mom." Well, this made me feel a little better, but I still fought off hard feelings over all the mean ways she'd treated me.

Many years later, one night I could not sleep, so I got up and went downstairs in my home to our comfortable couch and tried to get back to sleep. After much wrestling, I finally fell asleep, and I heard this voice say, *Pray for Elva.* If I hadn't spent the last several years getting my heart right with God, I doubt that I would have listened at all. However, even though I *knew* I'd heard that directive, I thought that maybe I'd been dreaming, so I lay there, waited and the voice said— firmer this time, *Pray for Elva.*

I responded, "OK, OK." But, I wasn't sure how much I could pray for her with my heart still so heavy with hurt feelings toward her. Then, I found myself praying with loving, kind thoughts for her, asking God to forgive her for all she had done, and to forgive me for hating her for so many years.

Early in the morning the next day my sister, Diane, called and told me that Elva had been diagnosed with cancer with only a few months to live. (Well, this explained the Christmas card I'd received the previous Christmas, where she had actually *written* in it saying she was sorry for all that she had done and that she really did love me. Yes, I tore that card up, too, telling myself that it was all lies!)

Now I realized that it was truly God Who had led me to pray for Elva. He led me to ask for forgiveness for her and for myself, causing my heart to soften toward her and have compassion for her. Remembering the Christmas card, I knew that God had moved in her heart, too, and allowed her to acknowledge an affection toward me. That is why she was able to write a handwritten note to me—for the first time in her life! The saying that tells us, *God moves in miraculous ways,* is right! God caused both of our hearts to forgive each other.

Elva, died a few months later, but I couldn't attend the funeral. I believed that Elva's and my shared bitterness toward one another had been healed, but her St. Louis family might bring it out in me again and I didn't want that. Even though recent events had softened our hearts and brought us peace, I knew that God was still working with me—bringing about a greater healing in my heart.

My son, Bryan...
Bryan graduated from high school and went to college. He won football scholarships, but dropped out and went into the *Air Force* where he did well, attaining the rank of Sergeant. However, drinking became a problem. Over many wake-full nights I agonized over the reasons behind addic-

tion. I considered what he had seen and learned from his Dad—and me—in his childhood. His Dad was a severe alcoholic, and I drank heavily myself. Counselors called it "self-medicating." So I concluded that Bryan had learned to handle problems the same way that his parents had—that was by drinking. "The drink" would make life's pains disappear.

By now, prayer had become a BIG part of my life, and I talked with God about everything! My prayers for my son flew out to God on a daily basis: "Please, Lord, help my son. Help him overcome the desire for alcohol, and any tendencies toward addictions."

It wasn't very long before Bryan was able to overcome his addictions. He was led to spend one whole year in silence—with no verbal communication—during which he only *spoke* with God! Through this spiritual experience he was delivered from alcohol, any desire for drugs and released from the pain of unforgiveness, rejection, abandonment and guilt.

Bryan and I are now closer than we've ever been, and I enjoy his companionship and counsel on a regular basis.

Bryan's High School Graduation Photo

His Dad, James, is much better, too, but still finds himself being weaned from alcohol. However, I see God healing his wounded heart, as James now knows that he was truly loved by his Mother, family, son, and me.

* * * * * * * *

Back to Arkansas...

Toward the end of my marriage-life-*dramas* with James—when I was about 27 or 28—I was able to make a trip back to Arkansas.

My brother, Joe Nathan, had removed our Mother from the mental institution and put her in a nursing home. She wasn't crazy, only beaten down, and unable to talk or express herself. When I arrived, she hardly recognized me, but in my heart I knew that she knew us—and seeing Joe Nathan brought a great smile. My brothers and sister and I recognized that she would never recover, but because of my brothers, Joe Nathan and Willie (who still lived in Arkansas), and their consistent willingness to look in on her, we knew that her last days would be happier. Willie spent many days looking in on our Mother and he also laid sidewalk and planted flowers around the Care Center to bring enjoyment and safety to all the residents. Joe would take Mother on frequent *outings*, and Willie helped Joe wherever he could.

Standing: JoeNathan/Hot
Sitting: Willie, Mother and me

My love for my brothers continues to grow, today, as I remember all the special things we've shared in our lives. The each bring a smile to my heart.

* * * * * * *

Forgiveness ? Are you kidding ?

I was beginning to hear that word everywhere! Of course, I heard it in Church, and most of the time those ministry-words-of-forgiveness fell into my category of *theory.* A nice idea, but nobody really forgives the awful pains and hurts like I had. Then I heard it from my family. My well-meaning sister, Diane, spent a lot of time talking about how *forgiving* people who have hurt us helps us "move on with our own lives." I could see the logic, but it just wasn't happening. When my co-workers started throwing that word around, too, that's when I got mad. "I don't want to hear any more about it!" I told them.

I knew that I needed time to heal and forget. But, FORGIVE? I couldn't even imagine it! Forgive? I wanted to kick James' ass and then kick it some more! Couldn't he see how much I wanted—and needed—my family to be together? After 15 years of trying—holding on in spite of the abuse, and going through two divorces—there was still a deep part of me that wanted to erase all the bad stuff, and turn those few precious, wonderful moments of marriage, and parenthood into reality.

Anger was also part of me—wrapped right around *unforgiveness*—and it seemed like one or the other surfaced in my life most every day. Oh, yea! I know a lot about *anger.* I had been mad—I mean **MAD**—for a long time before I ever thought of getting help. I remembered when I was 12 years old and my Dad died; he was all I had. Then they put my mother in a mental institution, and I was shipped off to a whole different part of the country! In many way's I'd been in charge of our daily household decisions, and then suddenly, I wasn't allowed to make a decision about anything. Yea! I was angry—hurt, fearful, and very angry—most of all at God!

There seemed to be so many pieces of my life that were not right—not what I wanted them to be, and I felt the effects of my anger is most every area of my life—from my general attitude toward people and my job, to my emotional connection with my own son. There was even a short time when I was so consumed with anger and unforgiveness that I ignored my own son. Some people might identify that at "having a big chip on my shoulder," and that *chip* really weighed me down.

Well, time did begin a type of healing. I did learn to practice a type of forgiveness and the persistent anger within me decreased. I'd come to a place where I started to smile again, not only on the outside, but also on the inside of my heart. Life began to grow in me again, and it seemed that I was ready for a *new* relationship. Would I ever marry again? I didn't know. However, somewhere deep inside me I believed that God's plan for my life included the *right* man.

Lesson I've Learned:

My dedication to my work (some would call it obsession), to my accomplishments, and to my son, kept me blinded to seeing the core problems in my life. I had created a pattern of survival that worked for me, kept a roof over our heads, and bread on the table. But, inside, I was empty, hurting, and walking on cut glass. I was so mad! I wanted to hurt people who had hurt me. I wanted vengeance! However, through wonderful family and friends—who had been praying for me—I found my way into counseling. I was finally prepared to *listen* and to work "it" out. I no longer wanted to just survive with all that buried anger and unforgiveness. After all, it had me *stuck in a rut* emotionally, physically and spiritually.

Meeting Ray
Accepting God's Marriage Plan

After I divorced my son's Dad the second time, I immersed myself into work, travel and teaching for hair manufacturers, serving as State President for our hair association industry, and still made time to visit my son's school, and sit on the advisory committee for his school. I was busy, and I *thought* I was fulfilled with positions, titles, money, travel, and an occasional boyfriend here and there.

There were several boyfriends who left good feelings in my heart and in my memories. But I was still lonely when I would come home; my son would go to bed, and it was just me. I would find myself feeling not just *lonely* but deeply alone in my heart and many nights I would cry myself to sleep asking God, "Why can't I find a good husband who would love and care for me and my son?" I felt like there was a big hole in my heart that nothing could fill—not even after all I had achieved.

Well, one Saturday evening my client and friend, Chauncy and I were talking and I asked him, "Do you know of any good black man I could date?"

Chauncy said, "Yes, but he's involved right now."

So, I finished his haircut and he went on his way. Then I finished blow-drying my friend, June's, hair whose hair was full, and wavy and I loved to blow it straight and give that uncontrolled/curly-hair a smooth look. All at once, the phone rang, and I was called to the desk. It was Chauncy, and he wanted to know if I would work in one more person. "No," I said, "It's Saturday, and I want to go home."

"Please." It was his brother, and he needed a haircut.

"OK, but he'll need to come right over."

And, right over he came! I saw him coming down the steps, and I loved the *jingle* in his walk. It was pure excitement as I watched him enter the salon.

I began his consultation, and hair cut, and I said, "Ray, I just want you to know that I don't date my clients." WOW, I thought, why would I say that? He hasn't asked me for a date. Was I just wishing to go out with him?

"Well," he said. "Great. I don't date hairdressers, either." My friend/client, June, was still sitting in her chair, and she and Ray began talking and quickly discovered that they knew each other from their childhood/school days. Then, Ray asked us girls (June and me) what we had planned for that evening.

"Just going to get a bite to eat," June replied.

"Well, maybe later you'd both like to come to a party," he said, and after giving us the location, he left.

I said to June, "I want to go that party, and get re-acquainted with him. He's cute, and I like his energy." I thought he was very sexy, too! Well, we went to the party and arrived a little early, and people were just hanging around. I thought, *What kind of party is this?* They just had beer, punch, and some potato chips and dip, with some kind of spread. *Kind of cheap,* was my first and lasting opinion! We waited and waited, and finally Ray arrived; I made it known that I was there, and he just kept hanging out with the fellows! That was IT! I was OVER the initial attraction! I stamped out, furious! How dare he invite us to a party and then ignore us? Ignore me! As I ran out, I ran my hand through my hair—my straight bangs—swung my head up and said, "GOOD NIGHT!"

Christmas was right around the corner and I was in need of an escort to our salon's Holiday party. I was the President of the Hair Association, and the only black (woman or man) at our salon, so I wanted a date who could talk, and hold a conversation, and look good...and that person was Ray.

I called him. "How was your haircut?"

"OK....Good," he answered.

"Ray, would you like to escort me to my salon's Christmas Party?"

"Hmmmmm," was his *enthusiastic* response.

"We're going to *Chez Thoa's* in Cherry Creek, and I know you'll enjoy the food; it's always great."

"Well......OK."

"Great." I was holding my breath, and about ready to scream.

"Do I have to wear a suit?"

"No, but dress up, because it's my salon's Christmas party."

Well, Ray met me at the salon, and he looked great! How proud I was to have him escort me. My female coworkers thought he was cute, too. It was great having him with me; we enjoyed energetic conversation and lots of laughter even if it was for only 3 or 4 hours. I found out later that he was involved with another woman, but he didn't know how to tell me.

Ray and I didn't get *serious* about each other for quite a while and continued dating other people. Then, one evening I experienced one of those make-it-or-break-it moments with my most steady boyfriend. I had cooked a great dinner for the two of us—stuffed Cornish hens, wild rice dressing and peach brandy sauce with all the trimmings—and he stood me UP! This man had done this before, and it was the LAST TIME! I was through! But, now I needed someone to eat with me—I wasn't going to let that great meal go to waste—and that someone was Ray. So I called him, and asked him to dinner.

"Well, I don't know," he drawled.

"We are having Cornish hens and dressing and great cake."

That did it. "Well, why not?" So, over he came.

I had all the intentions of having a wonderful evening with Ray, when all of a sudden the telephone rang, and my Doctor friend was calling to say he was sorry, he had to work late again. I said, "I'm sorry, too, but I have a friend over for dinner," and I hung up the phone—slammed it, to be exact. And that's how I met my Ray, and <u>my</u> Ray he was to be.

Well, I knew from the very first moment that I cut Ray's hair, that I wanted him as my husband and lover, and father for my son. We dated—went to great restaurants—and dated—went to the theater and art museums—and dated some more. After about three years, I began to press Ray about marriage. Neither of us were getting any younger, and I felt like we were wasting precious time living separate lives.

But Ray hesitated.

"Do you love me, Ray?" I asked one evening.

"Yes," he answered with a very absolute tone.

"Well, I love you, too, so let's get married."

Then Ray said, "I'll have to think about that."

What did he mean, 'think about it?!?!' He'd had three years to think about it! Well, Ray couldn't say why he wasn't ready—he just wasn't.

Time went on—and on—and I met his parents. They were a little shocked by my straight-forward approach and certainty that I was going to marry their son. So, I cooled it; at least I did my best to *cool it*.

GETTING ON...
...THE RIGHT...
...TRACK...

Most of my life, I felt like I was on the wrong *track* in my personal life, seeking love and acceptance and fulfillment IN myself or through sex, wine, money, position and recognition—only to find out these were just like Band-Aids, They only covered the scars, suppressed the pain, rejection, anger, hurt, and abandonment issues. When a brighter track comes into view, some unique events can occur to encourage us to move forward.

One day—after Ray and I had been dating about 2 ½ years—a woman named Marilyn Hickey came into my salon to get her hair done by Gary, her hair-stylist, and Gary introduced her to me. We had some small talk about my life, my church, and where I was at (that day) in my life. Nothing significant happened until several weeks later when Marilyn Hickey was in the salon again. We exchanged hellos and she left the salon after her hair appointment. However, on that particular day she turned around and came back down the stairs.

"Polly!" she said, "God says, *Life doesn't have to be hard for you, but you must give your whole life to Him.* I will see you at church tomorrow."

Not tomorrow, I said in my head, then repeated it out loud. "Not tomorrow. I have other plans." After all, this was Saturday night, and it was time to get-my-dance-ON, and on and on! The year 1987 was full of fun and DISCO and Saturday nights were my only time to participate. After dancing till I sweat my hair out, and white salt covered my skin, I would make my way home alone, starved for a pig ear sandwich with lots of onions, or tamales with lots of green chili! WOW! I was in heaven!

Many times, however, I would be so frightened to get out of my car at such a late hour in the morning—around 2 a.m.—because the people on the street were more than a little scary! But I would stand in line with the rest of the people and stare at them as they would stare at me. I guess maybe I was a little scary, too. This was my treat—from me to me—after a long week of hard work, diligence, long suffering, helping others, and just plain making it through the week. This would be my reward to myself, and dancing was a great way to escape, and escape I did, even if it was only for 2-4 hours; it was great! I loved it!

When I was on the dance floor, I felt like a queen. I could clear the floor, because people loved to watch me dance; WOW, what a great feeling! I would dance away all my troubles and anger for that evening, and I felt free. Sometimes I wondered if I shouldn't have been a dancer! But I love doing hair so much that I wouldn't trade a minute of it!

Well, back to Marilyn Hickey, and what she'd said to me—that she would see me in church the next day. *No way,* I thought. *Heck, I would be just getting home, and no way I could go to church. NO WAY!*

But <u>that</u> night of dancing turned out to be different. When I entered the bar as usual, with my friend Bill, I noticed the smell of alcohol made me want to puke. And the bar was so smoky that my eyes burned. *What was wrong?*

"Do you notice these horrible smells?" I asked Bill.

"No," he said. "Everything smells fine to me. What's wrong with you?"

Without hesitation I told him, "I have to get out of here."

I guess I looked like I was about to vomit, so he took me right home, and boy was I glad to get out of that place. I thought, *how could I have ever liked that place?* It used to be one of my favorite spots.

Well, I went to bed early and arose with a deep desire to go to church. So I got dressed and headed for *my* church; but no, I had a feeling deep inside of me that I needed to be at Marilyn's church that day. I also had this sort-of premonition that when I arrived there, there would be no seat for me downstairs. So, I argued with God. *I can't go way out there to that church; it is way on the other side of town!* But the urge was so strong, off I went, and upon arrival I tried to enter the main floor. Just like I'd thought, the usher said, "Sorry, no seats—we're full downstairs today!" Well, I was so mad after driving that far and no seats. But as I turned away the usher said, "There are seats upstairs." So I headed upstairs and as I was looking around downstairs I saw Marilyn on the platform, ministering, and she said, "Good morning, Polly! I'm so glad you're here!"

My immediate reaction was, *why point me out in front of all these people?* I didn't respond, but quickly sat down and read the bulletin. Well, at the end of the service Marilyn had an altar call and said, "If you haven't given your life to Christ, come down." That wasn't me. I had already given my life to Him when I was 36 years old, and now I was 43. Then she said, "If you feel like you have back-slidden...." *No,* I thought, *I haven't backslidden. I go to church when I feel like it.* Then she said, "If you want to be baptized in the Holy Spirit, with the evidence of speaking in tongues...." *No, I* thought, *Jesus didn't speak in tongues, so I don't need to either.* So, I didn't respond. But she gave one more altar call, "...for those who are wounded and feel that life is so hard, come forward, we want to pray with you." Well, I jumped out of my seat and went to the altar where Marilyn prayed over the group of people who had come forward.

Then we were directed to the back room for further prayer with Art, the head prayer-counselor. Well, Art spoke with me, and he asked, "Do you want to be baptized in the Holy Spirit?"

"I don't know. What was it?"

"It's the power of God working in you and for you," he explained. "Do you want to speak in tongues?"

"No!"

"Why not," he asked.

"Because Jesus never spoke in tongues and if He didn't need it, neither do I."

"Well, Polly, if God wants you to speak in tongues, will you?"

"Of course, but I know He doesn't. But if He did, I would be open."

So off I went and stopped by Ray's home, which was near the church. I shared the good news with Ray that I'd given my life to God and I talked with him regarding this *tongues* thing. Ray told me how he received it, and how this connection with the Holy Spirit was a deeper part of his personal relationship with God.

Well, next Sunday, I was back at <u>*Happy Church*</u>, and Marilyn and her husband, Pastor Wally said, "Polly, come to the altar, we want to pray with you."

"With me?" I said. *Why me, God?* I screamed out inside of me. *I can't be the worst sinner here! I can't be! Why pick on me?* But when I arrived at the altar, it was totally different than what I had thought.

Marilyn said, "Polly, God has called you into ministry!"

Me? I thought.

Marilyn then prayed over me, and assigned me to Mary Ann who became a wonderful prayer partner, and who (later) gave Ray and I one of the most wonderful gifts we'd ever received—our wedding reception!

That day—and those moments of prayer—were huge eye-openers for me. I *knew* deep in my heart that *God* had told me that He wanted to use me. ME! Through Marilyn and Pastor Wally, at that altar, God gave me a clear message that I could not ignore. It was suddenly so obvious to me— that God truly knew me to my very core and that He wanted to use the abundance of love He saw there—the love that I'd almost buried. I also realized that He would use my boldness.

So I began to pray and ask Him what He wanted me to do. The abundance of LOVE in me? Heck, I didn't know what that was—didn't believe I'd ever experienced *real love* so how could there be an abundance of love in me? All my life all I ever wanted was to feel and receive love. Now God tells me that I have an abundance of love in me—for others? How could this be? How?

Lesson Learned...

Even though Ray and I had been dating several years, we hadn't starting regularly attending the same church. We'd discussed our beliefs on a surface level, but both of us held on to OUR way—OUR church—OUR set understanding of God, and His place in our lives. Through these events in my life, I suddenly realized that God was more real than I'd ever imagined. He cared about me. He cared about Ray. God was working through other people to show us His love, teach us about loving each other, and about loving others, too. Now my *schooling* was really beginning.

* * * * * * * *

BIG and Little Steps...

Well, not very long after that, I volunteered to work in the prayer center at *Happy Church* and pray for other people. One day while we were there, the room was quiet and the head of the prayer room said, "Polly, God wants me to talk with you regarding going to Bible College."

Bible College? No way! I thought, *no way*. "I own a business and I can't go to Bible College. I'm just trying to get my business off the ground. How could I take time away from my business to go to classes or study?"

"Well," she said, "God sees you working part-time and going to Bible College part-time." So, I went to my Salon and announced to my receptionist that I was going to Bible College. I decided I would go to classes two days a week, and three days I'd work in the Salon. And, that is exactly what happened—for SEVEN years—yes, it took me seven years to graduate from a 2-year program. AND, it was worth every effort!

I loved Bible College! But the homework was huge and it was very challenging for me. The *cleaning up* on the inside of me was tough, as God was taking out the old and putting in His Love, His Word, His Character. He was healing me from years of rejection, woundedness, low self-esteem and unforgiveness, just to name a few things. The list goes on, and on, and on. Oh, yes, He had to show me who I was IN HIM and that I was not *what* I'd been told I was by others. People had been telling me for years that I was not a capable person, that I was insecure, and that I would never be able to achieve my goals. Now, I was beginning to see a *new* picture of myself and I loved it!

Lessons Learned...

As God began to teach me *who* I was in Him, He showed me that I was loved <u>because</u> He is love; He dwells in me, and Love dwells in me—not only love, but the *unconditional love* of God is in me, and therefore I'm loved. He also showed me that He has always accepted *me*, but not the bad (or sinful) things I do. God taught me to separate *who* I am on the inside from the things I do, because I can change the things I do.

* * * * * * *

Me and My BIG mouth...

One day, Marilyn Hickey (from *Happy Church*) came into the salon to get her hair done. As we talked, she asked me if I was married.

"No, but I'm dating this great guy who doesn't seem to want to marry me."

"Why?" she asked.

So I told her the whole story about how Ray and I met, and that my pastor, Pastor Liggins of *Zion Baptist Church* in Denver, advised us to "share church services at each other's church until God directed us." Then I added that Ray had been a member of her church—*Happy Church*—for years.

"Well," she said, "I guess I'll just have to look into who this Ray is," and she did. Ray told me later that she had called him into her office for a meeting and had prayed with him; that God had already given him a word about a wife...basically quoting Proverbs 18:22 to Ray: *"He who finds a wife finds a good thing, and obtains favor from the Lord."*.

That good thing was me! I had loved Ray for a long time now, and I wanted to be married to him and look after him and take care of him. After all, I was good at looking after people. I had a lot of experience! I had looked after my Dad, Mom, brothers, my sister's children, and my son. Now, I wanted to care for and love Ray for the rest of our lives.

Well, a few more years passed, and Ray still hadn't popped the question! So, one Sunday after church services at *Happy Church*, I took him to the altar to get prayer from Pastor Wally.

Pastor said, "Polly, if God wants Ray to marry you, He will work it out," and he said a prayer as we dashed off.

I remember how disappointed I was. But Ray was furious! *Livid* to be exact. He drove me to his home to get my car and did not invite me in. So, I went home knowing that our relationship was finally, totally, completely over.

I went to work the next day and told my receptionist that my future with Ray was over.

"How do you know?"

"Judy, he was so mad, and he hasn't called me yet."

Well, the week went by and I didn't hear a word from Ray. But on Saturday of that week, Ray called and asked me when I would get home. I said, "The usual time, around 6pm." "OK, I'll meet you there." Well, I knew in my heart that we were through, so I prepared myself, and drove home with a parting blessing from Judy.

When I arrived, he was sitting on the front steps and I said to myself, *Oh, no. I'm finished now for sure!* I was so nervous, yet I was still excited to see him. "Ray, it's nice to see you."

"You too," he said in his calm way.

"What's up?" I asked.

I hadn't even unlocked my front door before he said, "Polly, I would rather do anything but this, but God wants me to marry you."

WOW! I thought my feet would come right out from under me, or I would faint, or scream, and that's what I did inside. But I tried to keep controlled and calm.

Ray continued: "You probably will not want to get married when I do."

I thought, *Just ask, Ray! Quit fooling around and get to it!*

"I'd really like a December wedding—this year."

"Oh, no," I said, "not in December."

"See, I told you that you wouldn't like it."

"Oh, it's so cold in December and I really don't like red and white for wedding colors."

"I knew you wouldn't agree!"

Now was a good time to soften the moment. I said, "Have you eaten?"

"No."

"Well, let's go to *La Hacienda* and talk about it." So, we shook hands and off we went.

Well, we came to terms on having our Pastor, Wallace Hickey, and his wife, Pastor Marilyn marry us; and if she was in town, we chose November 28th, that year, 1987. It was the most beautiful day of my life!

My brother, Dr. R. D. Rucker, came up for the wedding and he asked me a legal question. What last name would I go by? I didn't know. Heck, I was so busy planning the wedding and working I hadn't even given that a thought. "Well," I said, "business-wise I've been known as Sanders for almost forty years, and all my legal information is under the name of Sanders. Plus, I love the idea that I would have the same last name as my grandchildren. But I do want to be Mrs. Peterson. So," I said, "I'll go by Sanders-Peterson."

I called Ray, and told him, and he hit the ceiling. "What? After all that ruckus to marry me and you want to keep your last name?"

"No, I want to add yours to mine."

Well, he would have nothing to do with that! Here I was on my wedding day, and we were in a stand off. What would I do now? So I consulted with our Pastors and they recommended that I keep my current last name "for a short time." I left it with God, and off I went to get married.

The WEDDING...!

What a wonderful day! Our family and friends were there, and so were our two sons. **Bryan** was home from the Air Force, and **Sean**—Ray's son—was home from law school.

How proud we were to have them with us, and to give us in marriage to each other. Sean was Ray's best man, and Bryan walked me down the aisle—giving me to Ray in marriage. During our wedding ceremony, God gave us a promise from His Word for our days ahead with each other: *a three-fold cord in not easily broken. The cord of Faith, Hope and Love, and the greater of these is Love.* Oh, yes! And, that is exactly what has kept us together these many years—our Faith in God, and our Hope that God would help us in all the areas where we need it, and to soften our strong wills. His great Love kept us (and keeps us) in the tough times, too.

Mary Ann—my faithful prayer partner—gave us the most beautiful reception ever in her home in the prestigious <u>Denver Country Club</u> area. WOW! We had fresh flowers everywhere, a three-piece orchestra, and great food!

After meeting, greeting, eating and then enjoying the great music with our family and friends, we went off to enjoy our first night of marriage at the *Oxford Hotel* in Denver. A few days later, we returned to pick up the generous gifts from our friends and family, and we were on our way to our new home! That was when I moved into Ray's home…and, boy, that is another story!

Lesson Learned…

In those days and weeks just before our wedding, and our first days of marriage I learned that God is able to give us our hearts desire, even though we may try everything in our own human power to <u>make</u> it happen. I had to learn to let go and trust God—that He knows the best for us and that He wants us to enjoy the very finest. His best is even better than what we could possibly imagine; and He proved that to me by bringing Ray and me together.

Settling Into A New Home
A New Life

WOW! My new home! So I thought. The first day—after *honeymoon* and moving—that I was off from work, I started putting our wedding gifts away; taking Ray's old pots and pans down and storing them until he came home. I cleaned the house, and put up our new dish sets, towels, and started dinner. How excited I was—until Ray came home.

He immediately noticed the little things I had moved, and then went and looked at all our new things and had a *fit* over <u>his</u> things being moved. I quietly told him that I had stored his pots and pans (from his former marriage) in the basement, so that he could go through them and decide if he wanted to keep any of them. He started screaming and shouting, and my wonderful first full day in my new home turned *ugly!*

"What is wrong, Ray?" I asked. "All I did was make room for <u>our</u> things—our new things together." Ray could not believe that I would move *his* things without consulting him first. Well, it only got worse, and I mean *worse!* I felt like a visitor in my own home. Ray would not let me change even one thing, and I felt like I had no place for my own things. Where would I hang my clothes? He made no effort to make room in the master closet, so I made room in the hall guest closet. I literally had no place in this house to call mine.

As a new wife, I had no home and very little of *my* Ray—the man I'd grown to love and respect over all the years of dating. Within six months, I realized that I had married a person who wanted control of everything inside, as well as outside, of the home. So one day—after months of making sure I didn't move or disturb a thing—I moved a small vase. He noticed it immediately, and set it back "where it belonged."

I immediately cried out to God. *God, how can Ray notice such a small item shifting from one side of the table to another? How?* Well, now I knew that I had to do a lot of praying.

The intimacy part of our marriage was going sour, too. I couldn't get my husband to come to bed with me. I so desired to have him lie with me and hug me, and desire me. My need to feel love and acceptance had been enormous, and even though it had lessened in the very early days of our marriage, it was becoming less and less. I talked with him about it, and he had no answer; he would just get angry and become even more distant.

After about six months I was one hurt and lonely woman. Ray began to make up stories: his head ached, or he wasn't sleepy, or he wasn't ready to go to bed yet. So, I prayed and asked God for help, and made an appointment with one of our Pastors at church.

Pastor Mark told us that we sounded like the opposite of most of the couples who came in to see him. I said, "What do you mean, Pastor?"

"Polly, most men complain about the same things as you, and women complain about the same things as Ray."

I thought, *Are we weird, or what?*

Pastor Mark told us that Ray's control issues were unusual. To want control in the home, as well as outside—in his professional life—was unique. Our Pastor also noticed our similarities. Because I had had such extreme responsibilities all of my life, I had basically been trained to be the *head* of a household. So, Ray and I were experiencing the same kind of turmoil—and there we were, married, and feeling miserable. Pastor Mark prayed over us and sent us into counseling.

During the second Christmas season of our marriage, I heard myself tell my sister, Diane, that I had never used my key to my home. She asked me, "**Why?**"

"I don't feel like I have a real home," I told her, and hearing myself say those words threw me into a holy fit. I was letting out all the anger I had bottled up inside of me. When Ray got home I unleashed it again, and told him that I was not going to live like that, and he had to get over it NOW! And, I meant, NOW! After all, this was my home, too! As you might imagine, the war was on, and I mean ON!

* * * * * * * *

In the Midst of Misery...Ministry...

Well, can you believe it! Through all of this misery and upheaval, we had opened our home once a month to help others. We would scream at each other—curse each other out and slam doors. But when it was time to open our door to others from our church, we would put on our smiles and become the ideal little couple. HA! What a piece of fiction!

Ray would switch into his teaching role—and he was (and is) a very good Bible teacher. I would become the hostess. We both *loved* the people who came to the group, and they loved us, prayed for us, and we became good friends. I continue to be amazed and blessed by how God used our ministry skills to help others, even though we were going through such serious personal struggles.

One day I was home from work, and a person from our bank called: "Mrs. Peterson?"

"Yes."

"I'm calling to notify you that your home is going into foreclosure today."

FORECLOSURE! "You must have the wrong Mrs. Peterson."

"Mrs. Ray Peterson?"

"Yes." I answered again.

"You are $7,000 in arrears and your home went into foreclosure today."

As calmly as I could, I thanked her, hung the phone up, and called Ray inside — he had been working in the backyard. I told him what she had said. "What's going on, Ray?"

He started screaming at me. "I didn't tell you because I knew you would react just *like this*."

"Ray, I'm going to strangle you! Are you crazy? How could you not pay our mortgage?" After all, I was paying half every month, and now I wondered what had happened to all the money I had given him? He never told me.

I just threw a fit, and I mean a FIT! What would I do now? I tried to think it through and wondered if I could borrow enough through my business to at least hold off the bank. But, my business didn't have it to loan us. I said, "Ray, what will we do now?"

He had no answer, and he just withdrew from me totally.

Oh, yes, we still had our next group meeting, and I told Ray that I would get them all to pray for us. Oh, NO! He didn't want anyone to know he'd lost our home. He wanted everything to look like we had no problems at all.

I hated the pretense; I hated covering up with lies and deception. Well, I promised him that I would not tell our group; but our home was still lost, and we had no place to go.

As was our regular pattern, Ray divided the group into two's when it came time for prayer. Now it was my time to get some help; I had strong faith in prayers of agreement. So, I didn't tell my prayer partners that we had lost the house, I just said I needed prayer because we had to move, and we couldn't seem to find a home. I also told them that we would have to move quickly. I felt terrible inside that I couldn't be honest with them. But I had given Ray my word.

So, as we were praying, this one guy—who looked and dressed like he was stuck in time—said to me, "Polly, I see God bringing you a home, a mansion. No, not a mansion, but you will feel like it is a mansion, and you'll recognize it by the detached garage. You'll love it!"

Well, I thanked my prayer group, and we all hugged, said we loved each other, and went our ways. Oh, yes, my group was a little "out there," but I loved them, and they loved me. We were very accepting of each other, and didn't judge each other.

Ten—maybe fifteen—days was all we had left to find a home, or we would be homeless. So Ray would look as he drove around town in his work/Utility Company van, and I would occasionally take off work and go with him. We never agreed on any of the houses we saw. Our tastes were so different—just like our Pastor told us on our wedding day.

We were down to our very last day. I took off from work and went with Ray, and told him, "Ray, if we can't agree this time, I'll get my own place and you can get yours!" I was so hurt, angry and frustrated, that I didn't know what to do next. I hadn't even started packing.

Out we went! *All of these homes out here, God, and we can't find <u>one</u> we both like?* By the time we returned to our neighborhood I was crying so hard I couldn't even see. I wasn't sure which of my painful feelings was greater; all I knew was I had to find a home. I was running a business, and I had to be in a secure place that I could call *home* and have some stability.

Well, Ray stopped the car in front of this great big house just three blocks from our house. I said, "Ray, why are you stopping here? You know we don't live here."

"Polly, you probably won't like this place either, just like you haven't liked anything so far!"

I just sat there and shook my head. Finally I got out, blew my nose, and wiped my tears, and when I opened my eyes, I said, "WOW! This is great!" Well, we could only see the outside, but I loved the color of the house; it was my favorite color for a house, gray/white and trimmed in burgundy. The yard was fenced in and private and it had a lease sign on it! "Ray, please go tomorrow and see it, and if you like it, go ahead and lease it." I knew that if Ray found it acceptable I would too, because I already liked it from the outside.

Well, the next day, I could hardly wait until I came home and to see what Ray thought. The minute I walked in the door I asked, "Well, Ray, what did you think about the house?"

"The man is prejudiced, so we won't be leasing from him."

"And, what else?" I asked.

"I think it's too big for us, and you won't like the kitchen."

"Why?"

"It has blue wallpaper, and yellow birds on the wall!"

I thought, *Is that all?* So, I asked, "What were they asking to rent it?"

"$1,500, but that is a little steep." (We were paying $1,250 for our last home.)

"Ray, I'll go and take a look at it tomorrow, on my day off."

So, the next day, I walked over, praying all the way, and I thanked God for that house and asked Him to make a way for us. As I arrived, my heart jumped, because I just *loved* the outside. I walked into the home saying, "Hello! Hello! Anyone here?" And I also hollered out loud, "I love this home! Oh, my God, I love this home. Hello! Hello!"

The house was Victorian, natural wood floors, French doors in the entrance, and natural wood steps leading to the upstairs. As I walked into the parlor—*OH, my God!*—I could hardly breath.

The lady of the house came out from the kitchen and said, "You really like this house?"

"Oh, yes, I love it!" I told her we needed a new home, and where Ray was employed, and that I had a small salon in the neighborhood, and that we were responsible individuals and had good references. After all, I had great friends, and well-known clients in Denver, and I knew they would help me. US! So, I asked her to rent to us.

"Polly, I told my husband I would not rent to anyone who didn't love my home."

"Well, *I* love your home, and I will take good care of it." She showed me around; I loved all the extras she had put into her home—soon to be my new home!

The very next morning, as I was walking, I decided to walk by and pray over our new home, and the Lord spoke to my heart: *Polly, you see that **seven** on your house.* I looked and I thought, *God, I don't see any seven. God must be blind.* But I didn't say that out loud, I only thought it. Then God said, *Polly, add it up.* So I did, and He was right. The address was **115**, and I said, "Yes!"

God then told me that this is where Ray and I would become ***one***, and where we would ***be completed***. (I found out later that the number seven in the Bible means completion.) And then, God said, *Polly, look up.* I did, and I saw the detached garage, and knew right then and there that this was my *mansion*. Till this very day, I love my mansion, and I so thank God for working it all out for us.

Our Mansion

Oh, YES! We were able to <u>buy</u> our home after leasing it for about five years. God made a way for us! He gave me a plan. I called the owner and asked about buying. She told me that she hadn't thought about selling, and I assured her that if she ever did, we would buy it.

Well, one day, after I'd almost forgotten about that conversation, the owner called. "Polly, my husband and I must sell the house in order to buy the real estate where we're living now." She asked me to get a market assessment of our house, which I did right away. Then we made an offer. There was a little negotiating—her husband saying that our offer was too little, but after a few weeks she called me back and gave us the house at its market value. I know that God helped her see how much we loved that house, and that had always been important to her.

I so thanked that woman. I cried, and I thanked God for helping us get our mansion! Ray loves his mansion, too, and he is a great caretaker of it! Everyone says he has the prettiest home in the neighborhood, and I agree! Now, we have a home that is OURS. We still share the mortgage, and we are still working on becoming *one*.

Lessons Learned...

Once again, I learned that with God all things are possible. ALL THINGS! Even when my husband and I were going through a season of barely communicating, and we felt like we were about to lose our home, possibly even our marriage, I found that God is faithful. Somehow, we moved past hurt feelings, and defeating circumstances to walk through the door of our new home.

This was also one of many opportunities I've experienced that helped me hone better listening skills. Although I have the natural ability to hear what people are saying, I've discovered that I'm already solving the problem before they're done speaking. Truly *listening*—sort of between the lines—has helped me understand my husband and myself better, as well as those people who God places in my path.

Becoming One
Gripping the 3-Fold Cord

This chapter deals with events that occurred during our 3ʳᵈ-5ᵗʰ years of marriage, and Ray and I just celebrated our 20ᵗʰ Anniversary. God never deserted Ray or me. Instead, God turned those things that could have been used for our destruction into stepping stones that have allowed us to minister to one another and others. God loved us through the rough stuff and continues to love us, building our marriage relationship.

One thing I've learned in my life is that as we, ourselves, must continue to learn and grow and so must our relationships, especially our marriage relationships. We cannot remain stagnant or we will wither and die. I'm discussing difficult issues in this chapter. However, the important thing to know is that God pulled us through it, and continues to heal our wounds, make us stronger and reestablish trust.

*O*NE? I thought. *How could this ever be God?* It seemed that our marriage—our one-ness—was falling apart almost the minute we stepped out of the honeymoon hotel.

Yet, I held on to hope, and the Power-Piece of our three-fold marriage cord, God!

During a conversation with a minister friend, she shared a personal example about the struggle for unity in her own marriage. When I walked away, I began to understand the truth behind the saying that *to whom much is given, of him much will be required.* My friend told me that once she and her husband stepped into their ministry great discord came into their married lives—yes—GREAT disagreements. "The only way to overcome this," she said, "is to be obedient to your personal ministries—*plural*—your ministry to your husband, and your unique outreach ministry, and pray."

Well, Ray and I both had God in our hearts. We were constantly fed God's Word through our church and personal study, and I felt like I had the *praying* part down pat. I believed that I had an "outreach ministry" through my hair-stylist gift. But…did I know *how* to minister to my husband? Previous experience was telling me that everything I tried, didn't work then, but Ray is a man of God and I am definitely a different person. However, as the months and years of our marriage progressed, I learned that we *saw* God differently. I saw Him as loving and forgiving, and Ray saw Him as loving and with rules.

Well, I found out that God is all of what we knew Him to be and more. He *is* love, full of compassion, mercy and grace. God also has *rules* for us to follow, principles that help us live excellent lives, discover Who He is and help us avoid trying to *rule* Him. If we're all honest with ourselves, we'd acknowledge the many times when we tried to tell God what to do. Shucks! Even knowing His rules, we still try to control Him and make deals with God.

For some time I had been asking—well maybe *telling*—God to FIX this marriage! After all, He had spoken directly to Ray about marrying me, so WHY were things so difficult! Our home-life seemed full of anger, rejection, pain, and severe separation. We were experiencing the kind of division where neither person leaves the home, but there is *separateness* within every room. Same house, but separated hearts—separated emotions—going our own ways.

Every Sunday in church I would *cry* (God might have called it *whining*), and ask friends to pray with me. They would console me, pray over me and with me, yet lots of time passed and nothing seemed to be happening.

Then one day, my counselor told me that I had more hidden anger than she had ever seen. *WOW*, I thought. This pretty little blonde has never seen anything if she thinks I'm the worse case she has seen. Heck, I was calm around her. But I knew that she was probably right. I'd been screaming at God for a long time—angry and hurt about my Mother's illness, and my Dad's death—about the pain of my first marriage, and all grief that spun out from it—and now the man I truly loved and was married to, didn't seem interested in me at all. Yes, I could see it now. I was mad—REALLY MAD! Beneath all my smiles and laughter, I was still mad at the world. Guess that makes for a challenging marriage partner.

One Sunday, the altar was open at church, and I went and lay at the altar and cried out to my God, *What is the problem with me, Lord? I thought that I had forgiven everyone You asked me to, way back when You dealt with me about anger and unforgiveness before. So, what is the problem, now?*

Well, I've known people who have heard the audible voice of God, and that day I did, too! I heard Him say, "Polly, you are still mad at Me."

"You are right," I said, "because You <u>could have</u> changed things and helped me and my situations, but NO, You just left me alone. WHY?"

That's when I felt a warmth like I'd never felt before, as if He began to cuddle me, and put His arms around me. "Polly, as you have forgiven everyone else, you have to forgive Me, too, and then I can help you. Right now, my daughter, I want to help you, but you have My hands tied, and I can't because it is sin to not forgive *Me*, as well as hold unforgiveness against others."

WOW. Right then and there I cried out to my God: *Forgive me God! Forgive me for holding all this anger against You and forgive me for holding all this anger against my husbands, my family, my mother-in-laws, my work associates who betrayed me; and forgive me for all the unforgiveness I have in my heart—known and unknown—in Jesus' Name."*

Right then and there, God forgave me and the healing began! Oh, I felt so much lighter, and all the weights came off of me. Even my face changed showing less tightness, and I could actually feel weights coming off of me. I bet I lost at least 20 pounds!

Well, I wish I could say that was the end, but God knew it would take some time to get me to release *all* the anger/malice I had in me. So He allowed several other experiences to occur in my life, to see how I would deal with them. I didn't pass with flying colors, as I felt justified with the *reason* to hold a certain grudge or resentment. But God showed me that I had to let it ALL go and give all my disappointments to Him—to lay all my resentments and strife at the altar. One-by-one I had to do it—I was/am the only person who *can* do it—because God had taught me that if I wanted Him to help me, I must forgive. I MUST! So, I would choose, with my own will, to forgive all of those who had lied and deceived me, and who had wounded me so desperately.

I also learned—in time—that true forgiveness does not mean that I forget the hurts, but that they no longer have a lasting affect on me. It is like having a baby: you remember that you had pain, but you don't/can't bring the pain back and dwell on it. Releasing anger, and practicing forgiveness is the same. I can recall the incidents, but I don't feel any of the pain; my heart is free. I can be kind and loving to all those who have hurt me and I can pray for them with the heart and will of God. That's when I knew I had truly forgiven—when I could pray with the heart of God for all of those people who had mistreated and wounded me so deeply. That's when I knew that with every bit of true forgiveness another rope was being cut from God's hands so that His helping hand could reach out to me.

* * * * * * * *

UNFORGIVENESS AT HOME...

The weeks of upheaval and uncertainty that surrounded our move into our new home—my *mansion* —brought out even more anger, unforgiveness and rage, things that I thought were dead and buried—so much so, that for awhile I wasn't listening to God at all. And then I began to suspect that Ray was having an affair. Although my heart was breaking, my main emotion was rage. That's right, rage! I wanted to kick Ray's butt! Many times I caught myself saying, "Ray, if I was a man, I would whip you till you bleed. How could you have an affair? How?"

I remember laying in our bed—alone—pretending I was asleep when Ray came home late, and listening as he cleaned up in the bathroom. Because of my experiences in my first marriage, I *knew* that when a man cleans up late in the night, it means he has had sex and came home without cleaning himself up. I recognized the symptoms. In addition, I began believing that God was speaking to my heart that my marriage bed had been defiled. DEFILED! What exactly did that mean? When I looked up the word *defilement* in a Biblical dictionary—corruption/ruination/adulteration—I *believed* it was true.

During this same timing, I began having physical symptoms—bleeding/spotting—which my doctor diagnosed as

STD (sexually transmitted disease) related. "How could this be," I said to God. "How…when all I had done was love Ray, and try to be a good wife?

By now, the evil spirit-of-fear had a firm hold on me. One of my very worst fears was that my husband had had an affair with a man. There was even a man calling the house and leaving a pleading voice message for Ray to call him. I had heard this voice several times and the spirit-of-fear was working overtime to convince me that Ray was gay. Well, who could I talk to? Who? So I called one of my pastors and he prayed with me and told me if Ray was gay he couldn't tell by the Spirit of God. But he suggested that I have Ray tracked by a private detective. I never did this, as I don't think I was ever ready to find it out, plus I didn't have the money.

Instead, I found myself following Ray in our neighborhood to a local restaurant to see who he was meeting. One day after work, fear grabbed me so tight that I was frantic and running up and down Broadway to spy on him. Finally I got a grip on myself and said, "Polly, look at you! You are like a mad-woman, running up and down the street, barefoot. What if your clients see you!" Well, I caught myself and I called a former friend who told me that if Ray was gay he would have seen him out in the bars—and he hadn't—so I better just calm down. YES, you can believe me, I am a witness to how **terribly** the spirit-of-fear can attack a person!

I then called out to a female pastor who told me her story, how her husband, also a pastor, had been gay all during their marriage and she only found out after he caught aids, and died. Well, that was the last thing I needed to hear, and it wasn't until much later that I realized the spirit-of-fear had directed that whole conversation.

Finally, I turned to God again and said, "God, if Ray is gay, just tell me. I can handle it now." Well I went to church and there was a visiting prophet of God speak that day.

That prophet just kept walking around my chair and saying, "Satan is a liar! He lies…he lies…he lies!" Well I knew and the pastor and his wife knew what he meant and my heart was so relieved. I KNEW right then and there that my Ray was NOT gay! Satan had been working in my mind, wanting me to believe he was—wanting to destroy what God had put together. The enemy will stop at nothing to destroy what God has put together. Remember, the enemy wants to destroy the goodness of God. By lying, deceiving and even trying to kill us and end our relationship with God.

What I learned…

Our *minds* can and will play tricks on us and cause us to believe wrong/hateful things about a person—even the people we love most. But God is TRUTH and His Divine revelations set our minds, hearts, and emotions FREE! Thank You, God, for sending that Prophet just for me. Thank You for freeing me from the spirit-of-fear, torment and destruction. Thank You for freeing my husband from torment, shame, guilt and from the spirit of unforgiveness toward me and himself, and for reestablishing trust within us for each other and with You.

About the adulterous affair: My husband told me that his doctor said the STD came from a virus and I finally chose to let it go and trust God to heal our hearts, marriage and home—and so God is!

* * * * * * *

HOW I HAD TO FORGIVE…

First I had to receive forgiveness for <u>myself</u>—acknowledge my un-examined reactions and forgive myself for opening the door to the spirit-of fear. I was led to study how easily our minds can be deceived, and I began praying again.

It was in and through my prayer time that God finally calmed my heart.

Then I was commanded by God to forgive Ray, but I didn't have to stay. When there is adultery, we are free to divorce as the marriage vow/covenant has been broken. But I prayed and prayed and said, "God, you know my beginning, middle and end. If I can not truly forgive Ray, then remove me from my home and marriage." I didn't want to put myself into a prison—a self-made prison. I had met women in my counseling sessions who had done just that—put themselves in a prison of no joy, peace, laughter or life. No. I said, "God, help me to make the right decision for me and Ray."

Well, after months of prayer and allowing God to heal my heart and to work with Ray, I decided to stay in my home and learn to re-focus my mind, re-love and re-trust Ray. I set out for a second time with counseling to get practical help I needed to rebuild my home, my broken heart and marriage. My final word to God was, "I would re-try, and re-open my heart of my own free will." But I would also set boundaries for myself. If Ray had another affair I would leave him. Because, then I would know he was not repentant, had not had a heart change, or even wanted to change.

At the same time, I also thanked God that Ray DID want to change—and did change! Ray allowed God to *break* his heart. God forgave him and reached out to re-establish His great unconditional love for Ray—His forgiveness and open arms—to say, "Son, I forgive you. Now go and sin no more." That's how *good* God is to us!

It would have been just as sinful or bad for me to live with Ray in unforgiveness as it would have been for Ray to have outside sex. Ray and I both had to learn to walk in forgiveness—re-learn and re-open our hearts for each other. We had to make that choice with our own free will.

During one time of prayer, God told me, *"If you choose with your will, your heart will follow."* And that is exactly what happened. I know it sounds too simple, yet I've come to understand that the medicated salve to heal those jagged, and bleeding wounds-of-the-heart is labeled *forgiveness*. With forgiveness and *in* time…my heart has healed.

As I spoke to myself about showing my husband mercy and grace, I was able to walk in true forgiveness. But I won't gloss over the process; it took <u>time</u>. Then God taught me to let go of ALL the marriage disappointments—past and present—ALL the hurts, rejections, and pain, and to give it ALL to Him. Again, I had to <u>choose</u> to let go. In my own natural will I wanted to hold on to every ounce of anger, not give it to God, because I *wanted* what I perceived to be *justice*. But one day, I physically handed the whole mess to God and said, "Please take this from me!" I was all in knots on the inside, and full of such painful rage that I was ready to explode. I felt like I had a cancer on the inside of me.

God's quiet voice said, "I will help you, Polly."

* * * * * * * *

COUNSELING…

In order to *receive* counsel, my heart, mind and will, must be <u>open</u> to God's Word and His instructions. There must be a *listening ear* to <u>hear</u> what the Holy Spirit counsels <u>through other people</u>. I had to want to change.

One particular counseling session brought me instant insight, and continues to bless me to this very day. I was confessing my struggle with unforgiveness. Ray had hurt me deeply, so deeply, and sometimes the silliest things would cause me to flare-up at him. I didn't like it. I wanted the situation to get better. But I felt stuck. That's when the counselor paused, and pulled out blank piece of paper.

"Polly," she asked, "do you believe you still love Ray?"

"I'm not sure."

"Well, will you let God's love flow *through* you, *to* Ray?"

"Sure," I answered, not really *sure* at all. "If God wants to do that, it's fine with me." I was barely willing.

Then she began drawing on the paper....

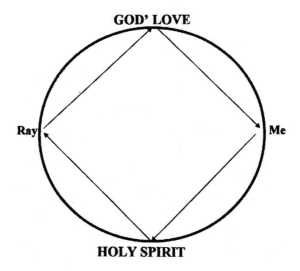

GOD' LOVE

Ray

Me

HOLY SPIRIT

Counselor Illustration

"Polly, it's time for you to <u>choose.</u> You must choose to love Ray again—or not." As she continued drawing, I could see a circle, and four words written at the edges. She turned the page toward me and said, "This is a visual picture of how God works *through* us."

The word GOD was written at the top, "ME" to the right side, the "HOLY SPIRIT" at the bottom, with RAY on the left side. As she spoke, she drew arrows—in a clockwise direction—leading from God, to me, through the Holy Spirit, to Ray and then back to God.

My own, personal studies in the character of God flew into my mind. God IS LOVE, and it is not *conditional*. It is unconditional, and so must I allow His unconditional love to reflect in my heart, my life, my marriage! So, there I was, taking the circle home with me, and putting it up on the door of our refrigerator to remind me of how God's love could flow through me, to the Holy Spirit, to Ray, and continually through God—for God loved Ray as much as He loved me. His love doesn't stop when we sin or let Him down.

Well, as I studied that circle. I knew that God loves Ray as much as He loves me! And, I just began to forgive Ray, out loud, everyday in my prayer times. God began to heal my wounded heart, and fill that deep void and hurt, with His unconditional love. I no longer felt isolated from Ray, the walls began to come down, and my loneliness was filled by God's Spirit.

As time went on, the Holy Spirit showed Ray that God had forgiven him and He still loved Ray very much. We cried a lot, and all of our anger, resentment and rages went away as we shed those tears and held each other and began to see each other the way God sees us—*forgiven* and LOVED and needing to be loved. Everyday, we still practice kindness with each other, respect for each other, and we are very thankful for all God has taught us and for all he continues to teach us. We choose to leave the hurts/failures behind us and start new every day—new with God's great unfailing love!

107

Ray—in front of our *mansion* home.

Peace and love is more evident in our home now and most important, peace and love flows in our hearts. We are learning to build trust in each other again and we know now, how important it is to forgive and let go. God is showing us our way with each other, and we are building a great friendship and rekindling our love for each other. I know our tomorrow-relationship will be greater than before, because God has ordained it, and we desire to follow His ways and His heart for each other.

* * * * * * * *

HIGHER ...Education...

From 1987 (the same year that Ray and I were married) until 1994, I was actively involved in the Bible College classes. That class-work not only gave me a stronger foundation in God's Word, but it also lifted me up, fortified me, healed me, and helped me grow (continues to help me grow) into the person I am today. What does this have to do with Ray and I "becoming one?" Well, I'll tell you.

Since childhood, I always felt like I would never amount to anything. I was just a little black girl from Arkansas who was only a "C" student. Who would ever care about her or about anything that she did? But over time, I discovered that there were some very special people who seemed to be *planted* in my life, who gave me the encouragement and *love* that I needed at just the right time. My Bible College instructors were some of those wonderful people, and so is my husband, Ray. Even through our emotional struggles, he has always encouraged me to learn more about God's Word, and "go deeper." I know that if I would have refused that opportunity, my life would be only a depressing shadow of what it is today.

Through those studies, and my prayer-time and relationship with God, He showed me how to separate the lies that other people told me about who I am, from *who* HE says I am. In His Word, God told me that I was born to be loved and to give love. After studying God's Character, I was able to develop an even deeper relationship with Him that has helped me understand His heart for me as His child. I was able to *fall in love* with Him and build trust in Him with the certainty of a child's *knowing*.

During my last days at Bible College, God spoke to my heart about yet another purpose/call for my life—showing me that He has given me a *pastor's* heart, and a *shepherd's* heart for the hurting and wounded people He brings to me. Throughout my whole life I have naturally loved and cared for people and what happens to them. Now God has equipped me so that I can give all that love and caring to them, as He does. And, as I give this love of God to others, I'm continually refilled, I can pass more love on to Ray, and I love it! I am so thankful for God healing my broken heart.

By the time I graduated from Bible College, I knew God's fulfilling purpose for my life. I was born to show the hurting and wounded that they are loved, that people DO care for them, and that they DO matter most to God. I was born to help them overcome their inner hurts, pain, rejection, low self-esteem, and to help them learn to forgive others, as well as forgive themselves. I was born to lead, teach and disciple others, and to build them to a point where they can become *who* they are meant to be. Then, as they learn this, they can pass all of this on to their children and their children's children, and to others. This way our *family* will know and experience love, and so will our communities wherever our reach takes us during all the days of our lives. Through God's great love comes healing, forgiveness, trust and healthy relationships!

Ray seemed to know these things about me all along. When we opened our first home for a small group Bible study, and I was hostess, Ray saw how people were blessed by the natural flow of God's love through me. Today, Ray continues to be one of my biggest supporters. I know that Ray's prayer support and involvement in my ministry is part of God's process in healing our personal, individual wounds, and in making us uniquely *one*.

Lessons Learned...

Although this whole section has highlighted a lot of the lessons I've learned, there is one lesson that I remind myself of every day. I am an incomplete God-*project*. Even when things happen that I don't understand, or I discover yet another flaw in myself, I **know** how much God loves me and that He is still molding me with His Mighty Love.

I saw a bumper sticker once that read, "Be patient. God isn't finished with me yet." I am so very thankful that He is forever faithful, and will never leave me in a mess.

SCREAMING At God!!!
Pulling the Splinters Out of My
Life-Lessons

As you've noticed in the former chapters, I've admitted to my bouts of screaming at God. For a portion of my life those tantrums were a daily occurrence—sometimes lasting a moment, other times much longer. Why ME, God? Why? Why? WHY?

➤ Why was I burned in that fire? Why did we lose our beautiful home?
➤ Why was my Mother stricken with that horrible illness? Why was I never allowed to *hear* her tell me that she loved me or have her take care of us?
➤ Why did I have to lose my Dad?
➤ Why did my Mother suffer such horrific treatment at the hands of medical people who supposedly had taken an *oath* to help people? Why, God, did you allow her to be tied to a chair for years?
➤ Why was I ripped away from my closest family— seemingly abandoned by my Grandmother—and sent far away? WHY?

> ➢ WHY did my marriage to James turn so ugly?
> ➢ Why did prejudice throw up so many barriers to my hair-styling career, and why did my career take so many sour turns?
> ➢ Why did it take me so long to find my *real* relationship with You, God?
> ➢ Why have Ray and I struggled so hard in our marriage?
> ➢ Why? WHY? WHY?????

One day—in the middle of one of my puddle-of-tears tirades at God—I fell into my chair, exhausted. I dried my eyes, my breathing became regular, and I sensed His presence.

You don't need to yell, Polly. My hearing is fine. I laughed! That's when *joy*—God's joy—started to really grow in my life again. I remembered that as a child, attending church every Sunday with my Grandmother Florence and little brothers at the Pilgrim Rest AME Church in Post Oak, Arkansas, I enjoyed wonderful singin' and preachin'. Then, when I moved to Denver I attended the Zion Baptist Church and listened to deacons read from the Bible, and heard ministers preach words that inspired me. I was married IN the church, twice. But it was not until the day that I felt God's presence—and His Great LOVE—that I ever really, truly, deeply, *believed* in Him. From that moment to this, I have devoured God's Word. I won't tell you that I've stopped screaming—because loud vocal tones seem to be just part of who I am, but there is a lot less of that. I've also come to a place where God is able to use me, to fill me up with His love and let me wrap my arms around the hurting.

I had been so *hungry* and *thirsty* for more of something all of my life. I had searched for acceptance and love in the approval of people, wine/drinking, astrology, etc. But when my screaming and pleading, and bargaining saw no results

I finally became still enough for God to reach me. I had no other place to turn to—none. So I turned to God and He revealed Himself to me and in me! Not only has *LOVE* done this for me, but I can now help everyone I meet to know that they, too are loved. They, too, have great value as a person. God accepts them right where they are! All you have to do is to desire to know Him in your heart and He will reveal Himself to you. His unconditional love for you awaits!

Because of His LOVE (and the counselors/friends/pastors He's placed in my path) I've learned that my life had been driven by the wrong things—hurt, pain, anger and resentment. All I had tried—in my own wisdom and strength—all the energy that I'd given, was never enough. All that I'd done *for* myself, was to *will* myself—push myself—to go on. I hid everything inside me, and built gigantic walls around me and in me. I submerged myself into my work and for a short time I almost forgot that I had a son who needed me. I continued to work and work—angry and disgusted with myself, and the world around me. I said, "God, why? WHY?"

Then I seemed to find a plateau—a place of OK-ness—and I re-emerged, allowed my heart to feel again, and I cried and cried and cried—and life went on. I thought I'd made it. I *thought* I'd come through those terrible experiences. I thought I'd left the rage behind.

However, I kept looking on the outside for something to fill me on the inside—professional success, drinking, parties, men—all made me feel good for a short time, but always left me wanting more. Like a car takes gas to *fill* it and make it run, those things kept me *going* until they ran me dry. I saw people "falling in love" all around me, and I continued to search for a certain man to come and love me. Then, I would be happy. WRONG! WRONG! WRONG!

WOW was I wrong. Even when a man of God came into my life (Ray), the *void* was not filled, because only God can fill that void, not a person. People are only temporary substitutes.

My Mother passed away in 1987, the same year that I re-dedicated my life to God, and the same year that Ray and I were married. Over the years, I became an adult and could fully realize the agony she must have suffered. There were many time when I literally beat the ground and screamed at God. Mother never recovered from the epilepsy or those horrible days in the mental institution, and she certainly never deserved any of those awful experiences. God has never explained *why* all that misery occurred. However, He has brought me to a place of peace where I can trust Him with my Mother's complete restoration and happiness, and I no longer *need* to know why. When God gives you His peace, it removes the *why's*!

I remind myself of these events in my life because, today, I *know* that God wants to untie us from our negative past so we can be free to live the bountiful future He has planned for each of us. He wants to set us FREE!

By God's design we are three-part beings—body, soul and spirit. He revealed to me that when we are physically sick or injured we see or feel signs in our bodies and seek help. There are also signs when our soul is sick or injured, but we don't always recognize them as easily. Some of those signs include feelings of low self-esteem, rejection, insecurity, even unresolved anger. When those pains/scars still have a *hold* in us, they lead to control issues, feelings that you can't measure up, or that you are continually being attracted to hurtful relationships.

Understanding this helped me realize why there were so many negative, painful relationship issues and conflicts in my life, and why I could not overcome them. No wonder I had no belief in myself and/or *wrong* beliefs (thinking opposite of God's Truth), and felt nothing would ever change for me.

When we feel tied up, or overpowered by these symptoms, we sometimes think we just need to be left alone and suffer. But what we really need to do is to seek God's help. God's Word in Luke 4:18 says: *"...He has sent Me to heal the brokenhearted, to proclaim liberty to the captives...to set at liberty those who are oppressed...."* God's promise to us is that He WILL deliver us and heal our broken hearts! However, we need to truly desire God's healing, be open to Him and allow God into our hearts.

Once I was willing to let the Truth of God's Word untie me from my terrible past, there were four basic steps I took to become *full* of His Love and promises:

1. I acknowledged that my soul was sick.
2. I quit blaming others, and looked at what I could do to make Godly changes in my life.
3. I sought God and asked Him to heal me in all the areas of my mind, will and emotions/heart.
4. I asked God to forgive me for all my sins—drunkenness, unforgiveness, resentment, anger—known and unknown sins—all of the things I held against others.

As I prayed and chose to apply God's love and Word over my life, my heart, God began the healing process—from the inside, out. If you, too, are willing to take these steps *with* God, He will heal your broken heart, too, and untie you from all the burdens of your past. Nothing is impossible with God! No matter how bad it looks! Nothing! Try God. He loves you *so much*!

Lessons Learned...

I now KNOW that my God is truly a wonderful, loving, caring God! His Love is powerful, unconditional and everlasting. Nothing can come between me and God once I have accepted/received Him into my life. His love will bring healing and health to our broken relationships, and He will cause us to have fulfilling lives—a life of abundance, love, peace/inner peace and health! Thank You, God, for letting me know You as *Love* and as *Emanuel*, my Friend.

Covenant House of Love PPS Ministries

As I write this book, I have served as President, Founder and Pastor in the *PPS/Covenant House of Love Ministry* for 15 years. Many broken hearts have been filled with God's love—living better lives, happier on the inside, as well as becoming able to help others experience that same love. This doesn't mean that life is perfect for all those who are touched by this ministry. It means that we now <u>know</u> we are loved and cared for; we can better handle the daily problems, circumstances, trials and situations that arise in our lives. It also means that we are not so *hungry-looking* on the outside because of the need to be filled with love on the inside. We've become rooted and grounded in God's love allowing our emotions and our-*selves* to grow in stability and confidence.

In Our Home...

PPS Ministries started in our home as I opened our doors two times a month to serve and help other hurting women. I shared my own life experiences, taught them about God's love and prayed for them. Sometimes like a flood, sometimes like a sprinkle of rain, they were able to open up their heart issues in that safe environment, know the Love of God, and allow the love of other women to reach out to them. They shared their hidden hurts, physical and sexual abuse, rejections, pains, fears, abandonment issues, losses, woundedness, and their heart's cry to be loved. I heard it time and time again: All they wanted was to know and experience love and the healing of their broken hearts and souls—just like me.

By 1994 (just after I graduated from the Bible College) this ministry grew into an outreach ministry—*Covenant House of Love*. Other women have come along side of me and we've provided luncheons where we taught, prayed, praised and worshipped, and had great food and fellowship. We've seen many women healed from their suppressed hurts and woundedness. We also created discipleship/mentor programs where women could call, receive prayer, and talk with another person, one-on-one, establishing healthy relationships with each other.

Then, we went to a larger audience through radio, TV and newspaper articles monthly, and we have seen many more people healed. The very *vision* God had given me was to *go*, and as I go, I see the great need for women—and men—to know God's Love and Healing power.

Accepting God's Call...

God is still calling, and I am still responding. I receive His Love, and He shows me how—in my own unique way—I can give His love to others. This is an ongoing process, one that challenges me often, yet blesses me always.

As you might imagine—after reading the previous chapters—*receiving* has not been one of my stronger qualities. However, as I began to walk-out my calling to give this Love of God to others, I discovered that I was able to not only give more, but that God's love was overflowing through me. Those who attend our meetings, outreaches, luncheons, or hear the radio program, or read an article are deeply touched—and their wounded hearts begin to heal.

At first it was much harder to be open and show love to those closest to me who had wounded me so terribly. But God gave me a lot of His unconditional love for them, allowing me to demonstrate His love through mercy, grace and forgiveness. That felt great!

To know and experience love is the very best thing you can have in your life, for out of knowing this we are fulfilled from the inside, no longer seeking titles, position, money, status, or just the right person to make us feel alive or loved. I know now that the great hunger for love can only be known from the inside of me, not from the outside of me. Instead of looking for love in business, other people, and achievements, I discovered that the love I so wanted came to me when I was ready to open my heart and say, "Help! God I need to be loved, to know Your love and to experience it from You, not only read about it a bit, but *know* it and *experience* it."

THAT is my *ministry*, my purpose in life, and what makes me *alive* more than breathing. What a wonder-filled gift God has given me! When God gave me *Love* (Himself), He gave me the very thing I longed for and desired all of my life!

Lesson Learned...

What I learned about *love* is that it is FREE! You can't buy it, or earn it, or sleep for it. Only by allowing and experiencing God's unconditional love will your broken, wounded, hurt heart be filled with His great love! All I had to do was to reach out to Him, ask God to heal my heart, and that void in my heart was filled! He is waiting to fill voids in your heart! When God fills the void in your heart, it doesn't mean that you won't feel lonely or that you won't reach out yearning to be held. When those moments come, yield your longings to Him and He will heal those feelings of loneliness, rejection, abandonment. *Love* does not mean that you won't feel pain. It does mean that *Love* is IN you. It waits to be given out and as you give, love will be restored in you and for you. God's oil-of-love never runs dry! Never! Never! Never! Because God IS LOVE and He is in you and His love is in you. Happy loving-days are ahead!

Remember: God loves you! Just as you are! He loves you even if you don't love yourself or if it seems that no one else has ever loved you, or even if you have failed in unloving relationships. Other *loves* may abandon you, but His unconditional, unceasing love will always be with you! Always! No matter what! Always!

Only God's love can overcome the hurts, rejections, abandonment, fear, abuse and woundedness you have experienced. My prayer is that your heart will be open, and that you seek/desire Him with all you heart, soul, and will. Remember, when you ask, seek, knock, He will reveal Himself to you.

Covenant House of Love
aka PPS Ministries

PLEASE FEEL FREE TO CONTACT ME AND LET ME
KNOW HOW I MAY BE OF SERVICE TO YOU.
My ministry includes: teaching, seminars, establishing
women's support groups, speaking engagement, special
conferences and other assistance as the Lord leads.

Polly Sanders-Peterson
PO Box 9727, Denver, CO 80209
ppsministries@msn.com or www.covenanthouseoflove
or, www.PollyandCo.com, 1.877-744-2122

EPILOGUE

I wrote this book as an encouragement for all who grew up feeling like I did, unloved, unwanted, unaccepted and never good enough. It is my hope and prayer that as you read about my life and see how God brought me from a place of believing lies about myself, to HIS Truth that He has always loved me, that you will find your way into His loving arms. It was my circumstances—and the *way* I looked at them—that created a void in my heart and made me believe I was unloved. As God helped me recognize and experience His unconditional love (1 John 4:16), I pray He will help you to discover how He loves and cares for you (Ephesians 3:17-19). He totally accepts you, *just as you are*. Psalm 139: 1-5 (TLB) has helped me understand that God *knows* me so deeply, yet still loves me and wants an everlasting relationship with me—and with you.

God's LOVE will cause you to overcome wrong circumstances/situations, heartaches, bitterness, rejections and insecurities that come against you. May your eyes be opened, your heart be filled with His GREAT unconditional, unceasing Love, and your lives become the very best they can be.

All my love, and His
Polly Ann

Tons of thanks

I simply cannot close this book without expressing my
"THANK YOUs" to a few of the most important people in
my life.

To GOD...

Thank You for loving me, rescuing me, teaching me,
healing me, and giving me peace. As You've helped me
grow in Your ways and character, I've discovered that You
were always there for me even when I couldn't recognize
You or hear You.

Thank You for allowing me to experience those feelings
of hurt, failure, rejection and disappointment, for without
ever knowing these, I might never have sought out Your
great Love and Your healing power. Thank you for removing
those boat loads of anger, pain and rage from my heart, and
for filling that void with Your true love! I know now that
You are Love, and that You loved me from the beginning of
time. Your love will always be with me—from now through
eternity! I will never, never, never be without it!

Thank You for Your Divine plan for my life within the
profession of cosmetology. You planted in me the gifts,
talents, abilities, and my unique personality that has given

me success in my career. WOW, God! I always wanted to own my own business and now it is a reality! Plus, I now have a national and international website that is growing day by day! THANK YOU GOD!

Thank You, God, for giving me my beautiful parents, and family; my awesome son and grandchildren, and my Ray. Without these people in my life, I wonder if I would have every found Your true love. I especially thank You for bringing Ray into my life and making a way for Ray and me in our marriage, as I continue to appreciate all the good qualities in him.. Please, Lord, help us to be persistent in become *deeply, and completely* one.

Thank You for loving me enough to teach me Your truth about forgiveness, and for helping me to forgive You and all the people who broke my heart. Now God, I'm FREE! It feels great, and I can forgive much quicker and easier now.

Thank You, God, for the Covenant House of Love ministry and for trusting me to love the ones who are hard to love. In this *safe place* I have the opportunity to share your miraculous healings from those past hurts with so many others, and show them how Your great, unconditional, unceasing love will heal their lives, their families, and their relationships.

One Last Word on Forgiveness…

To all those who may have wounded me, know that I forgive you; and for all those whom I've wounded and hurt, please forgive me. I'm deeply sorry for any hurts I may have caused in your heart and life. How can words ever say what is in my heart? For, without knowing God's unconditional love, I would be in the same place still holding on to unforgiveness, and still experiencing the same hurts. But, now I'm free—FREE to love with the love of God that He has put in me. I pray that you, too, may experience the same FREEDOM!

Father, God, I so thank You for Your great abundance of love for me and for others. I thank you for continually revealing Your unceasing love to all who seek and need it. Lord, I now ask You that all who read this book will come to know that You are LOVE and that Your love will fill their hearts, fill their voids, and erase their losses, now and forever.

Amen

Your daughter, Polly Ann

To Ray...

To my Ray: If I have forgotten that you are a gift from God, forgive me, and know that I'm reminded daily as I see you and know in my heart how thankful I am to have you in my life to share in God's love.

Thank you, Ray, for being my special someone to love in the good times and to cry with in the tough times. It is in those tough times that I believe we both grow the most and where I've learned to love God's way.

I believe that God has placed you in my life as my protector/provider and that your love for me reflects Christ's love for His Church (Ephesians 5:20). I pray that your husband-heart safely trusts me (Proverbs 31:11), and that as our love for God grows, so will our marriage-love grow and be strengthened, and that we will be friends and lovers always.

To Dad...

Thank you, Dad, for showing me the values of commitment, diligence, loyalty, good work ethics, how to be responsible, and how to reach out to others in need. And thank you for taking the time to walk me to the school bus stop, and other long walks that we shared. I know now that you really did love me and cared for me even though you didn't show it by hugging me or telling me — with words — that you loved me.

To Mom...

...who I only knew as my *Mom*, how beautiful you were! Your gentle heart, your caring eyes and quiet spirit showed me your love even though you were unable to speak. Thank you for knowing when you gave birth to me that I could continue to show your love to our family — as if your love for them was pouring out through me. During my childhood you surely showed me how to share love. Thank you for being my Mom.

To Bryan, my son...

Thank you, Bryan, for being the wonderful man-of-God you've become! You are a true testimony of a mother's heart being poured out to God, and His answer in showing you the way. Thank you also for my two grandchildren. God really knew I needed my son and grandchildren to pour my motherly love into. Without you, I would have missed out on so many wonderful things. You are the BEST son EVER!

To Grandmother Florence...

Thank you for being an example of *how* to love and care for others through taking care of me and my little brothers. I will never forget the work you put into cooking wonderful meals, making dresses for me, and taking us to church every Sunday. It is my hope that I might exemplify your endurance, patience, hard work, service and love for my own family and others as you did. Thank you for demonstrating God's love and care in my young life.

To Mr. Race…high school student advisory counselor…
WOW, Mr. Race! If you hadn't kept encouraging me to seek Beauty College classes, I would not have the career I have today. Thank you for your support and for giving me just the right amount of *push* in the right direction!

To Mrs. Rose…instructor at *Hollywood Beauty College*…
Thank you, Mrs. Rose, for caring, guiding and pulling out the gifts in me for people and doing hair. All your patience and willingness to go over and over the lessons with me until I finally learned how to make a finger wave—WOW—I appreciate that so much!

To Mr. Harry Lardano…director of the *Hollywood Beauty College*…
Thank you, Harry, for valuing me and honoring me as a person, and for teaching me that I could not let other people determine my worth. I had to believe in myself, and know I was as good as any other hairdresser, at the school, or anywhere. Your color-blinded-ness gave me a confidence that I really needed during those days of my life.

To Bryan's Grandmother Sophronia Pratt…and his Aunt Juanitha…

Thank you for being part of God's plan to make a way for me to work, while knowing that my son was safe and happy. Without you two in my life, I never would have made it.

To Miss Minnie…my 1ˢᵗ hair salon employer…

Thank you, Miss Minnie, for giving me my first opportunity to do hair. Your kindness, and the continuing *lessons* you gave me moved me forward in this wonderful career.

TO ALL my employers…

…who believed in me and taught me so much. For without your love and caring hearts, I would not have made it thus far! Thank you for sowing your gifts/talents into me and for helping me to reach higher and higher. You are the BEST employers, friends and co-workers ever! THANK YOU!

- ➢ Vera
- ➢ Phil Sanchez
- ➢ Christy Du Pays
- ➢ Erik and Rita Lobben
- ➢ Paul Garcia
- ➢ Gary Stratton
- ➢ Ted Garcia

To My Co-worker and Friend, Martha…

Thank you Martha, for all your love, support, and encouragements you've given me over ALL these years. You are the BEST, I love you, and so thank God that he placed you in my life. When I think of all the praying we've done together, I wonder whether God had time to listen to anyone else! I continue to pray that you, your children and grandchildren enjoy a good long life with each other, and that all your days will be prosperous!

To Mr. and Mrs. Jackson…our neighbors on Madison Street…

I believe that you literally *saved* my life, not only through all the little kindnesses, but for being willing to get involved and call the police at just the right time. Thank you! THANK YOU!

To Earl and his wife…my 3rd salon employer…

Earl and Helen, how can I ever repay you for all the love, care, giving and wisdom you taught me. I continually pray over your children and grandchildren, that they might be blessed because of what you sowed into me and so many others. Thank you, God, for that great open door, and for placing such wonderful, caring human beings in my life. And a *white* man, too!

To Michael Taylor...@ *Antoine du Chez* in Cherry Creek...

Thank you, Michael, for being patient with me and teaching me, and not giving up on me even when I felt like giving up on myself. Thank, too, for pushing me to let go and re-learn, and open my mind to greater opportunities. You are a true visionary and developer of people. Thank you! I pray that your days be long and prosperous, healthy and full of life—as full of love and giving as you are.

To my Beloved clients and friends...

Yes, friends, when God gave me *you*, He gave me the very thing I needed—YOU—to offer you my salon services, hug you, laugh and cry and share with you. THANK YOU for selecting me as your hairdresser and giving me many years (over 40, now) to go to a place daily where I was the happiest. And, I even made money, too! Is this great, or what! I love you and I'm so thankful for you. May God bring continued abundance, health and good life for you—your families/children—ALL the days ahead.

Wallace and Marilyn Hickey...founding Pastors of *Orchard Road Christian Center* (Happy Church)...

THANK YOU, Marilyn for drawing me to my God and to His great love. Also for all your love, care, wisdom, guidance and prayers. THANK YOU Pastor Wally for your great love, care and prayers, and for never giving up on me, and for showing God's heart to me. Thank you, too, for uniting Ray and I in marriage and blessing our home. Much love, Polly Ann

To pastor Norm and Jan brown...
Thank you for your heart-of-giving, for your care, and for taking the time to show God's love and healing power in my life. Thank you for reaching out and taking my hand and helping me to walk in the Love of God!

To Mary Ann...prayer partner, friend...
Thank you, Mary Ann, for all that you sowed into me, and for the great wedding reception you gave for Ray and me in your beautiful home. Your love and wisdom have showed me more of the love of God—like I had never experienced before. May you continually receive all of God's goodness for your life and your family.

To Bertha Lynn...Colorado TV anchor/journalist...
Thank you, Bertha, for all your love, help and great support throughout the years, and for the great advertising moments. And...thank you for looking so great all the time, showing off my hair-styling skills!

To Royalene Doyle...Writer, Editor, Legacy Hunter, friend...
Royalene, how thankful I am for your gift to write as if you were in my heart. Great job! Thank you for your encouragement, prayers and great love. Love, Polly Ann
P.S. You can reach Royalene @ *Doyle Writing Services*, www.doylewrites.com or royalened@netzero.com.

CPSIA information can be obtained
at www.ICGtesting.com
Printed in the USA
FSOW01n1626280716
23216FS

9 781604 777024